Forensic Fantasies

FORENSIC FANTASIES

Doctors, Documents, and the
Limits of Truth in Turkey

Başak Can

PENN

UNIVERSITY OF PENNSYLVANIA PRESS

PHILADELPHIA

Published by
University of Pennsylvania Press
Philadelphia, Pennsylvania 19104-4112
www.pennpress.org

Printed in the United States of
America on acid-free paper
10 9 8 7 6 5 4 3 2 1

Hardcover ISBN: 978-1-5128-2776-7
Paperback ISBN: 978-1-5128-2777-4
eBook ISBN: 978-1-5128-2775-0

A Cataloging-in-Publication Data record is
available from the Library of Congress

To my mom and dad

CONTENTS

Forensic Medical Documentation
as a Fantasy

On a cold December afternoon in 2011, I met with Dr. Burak, a professor of forensic medicine, at a garden café in one of the busiest neighborhoods of Istanbul to learn more about his expertise on forensic investigation of human rights violations. He was a sought-after figure among human rights activists and political groups because of his expertise. He had participated in mass-grave exhumations on behalf of the victims' families, prepared independent forensic expert reports on behalf of torture victims, and made public statements as a university professor supporting the ill prisoners' right to access medical care. On several occasions, he had testified against official forensic reports prepared by the Council of Forensic Medicine (Adli Tıp Kurumu, CFM)—the national forensic expert authority affiliated with the Ministry of Justice. I was curious to understand the role of forensic medicine and forensic doctors in detecting and investigating state violence in a setting where there was no dominant reconciliatory paradigm or transitional justice mechanism to address the consequences of state violence. Moreover, the pro–human rights forensic work of doctors like Burak had to compete with the legal, bureaucratic, and technical authority of the CFM. I asked him what he thought of the CFM and its importance. His response was sharp: "The Council of Forensic Medicine has been the washing machine for the dirty clothes of the state." For him, only the CFM—not the parliament, the media, the government, or the judiciary—was able to erase the stain on the clothes of the state—in other words, bloody consequences of violent acts of security forces and extreme or illegal uses of force including torture, kidnappings, or extrajudicial executions. Over the course of my research, this metaphor of "washing machine" frequently came up in the narratives of doctors who are working in the field of human rights. By this phrase, the progressive doctors implied that the CFM has been playing a central role in the state's denial regime vis-à-vis state violence.

Writing about colonial modernities, Ann Stoler (2002) argues that denial or rather, producing lies and silences, is intrinsic to governance. The manipulation or denial of facts have been integral to settler colonies, imperialist policies, nationalist and authoritarian projects, and liberal capitalist technocratic politics. However, lies, denials, and silences are not automatically enacted; rather, political and official denial is calculated and highly structured (Cohen 2001). They are created by complex systems put in place, which involve actors, experts, relationships, documents, circulations, and discursive norms. As this body of literature suggests, the systematic denial of torture is built into institutions, mechanisms, and practices that deal with the live and dead bodies that were tortured in Turkey. Yet, at the same time, phantasmal commitment to facts can be a strong pillar for the denial of violent acts while at the same time inspiring doctors in the field of human rights. Despite the accusations toward the Council and contentions surrounding its reports, forensic doctors are firm in their commitment to the truth and facts in their discourses. We therefore cannot understand the forensic denial regime without attending to phantasmal commitment to forensic veracity and scientific suspicion prevalent among forensic doctors.

As I followed the work of the progressive forensic medicine doctors in the last three decades as they formed alternative networks to forensically document state violence and reveal the hidden truth of state crime, I have begun to realize that their understanding of forensic medicine and what it is capable of as an expert technology has a phantasmal quality to it. It is this quality that have kept these doctors affectively tied to the human rights work and movement and helped them build their political and expert identities. Theirs is a fantasy about forensic medical practices and how forensic evidence in the form of medico-legal documents and reports have the power to detect and reveal the truth of state violence and even transform the latter. Over the course of my research, I have also realized that this is a fantasy shared by state officials, politicians, and political activists to different degrees when addressing the question of state violence and forming their political communities. This book brings forensic fantasies that animate diverse communities around forensic medicine in cases of political violence to the center of the political and theoretical inquiry into how life, death, and the human body are inscribed in the order of power in modern societies. I'd like to trace gray areas where state bureaucracies, officials, and human rights activists are equally captivated by forensic fantasies. This book thus tells the story of the relationship between human rights politics and state violence in the last three decades in Turkey from the perspective of how forensic fantasies have inspired doctors, state officials, and dissident groups simultaneously through a contentious politics of truth. These fantasies are generated and circulated not only through political actions, solidarity networks, and professional organizations but also through laws, regulations, or resolutions informing how diverse actors approach questions such as: What is state violence? When and how can state violence be classified as torture? What would be the legal and political consequences of producing medical evidence of torture?

Ethnographies of violence have long addressed the question of erasure, denial, evidence, and proof. The episodes of political violence such as enforced disappearances in Argentina or civil war in Spain are said to be characterized by systematic "efforts to conceal, disappear, and distort evidence" (Maguire and Rao 2018, 15). The right to truth emerged as a fundamental principle of various post-violence justice mechanisms such as reconciliation programs, amnesties, and memory movements that aim to address the legacy of massive human rights violations that are often built on regimes of denial (Cohen 2001). These mechanisms were designed to address past violence by uncovering the truth, with the underlying idea that without coming to terms with the truth about past violence, societies cannot heal, make peace, or envision a collective future.

Anthropologists have shown the expansive use of forensic expertise in search of the truth in human rights and humanitarian practices as well as transitional justice and post-conflict processes (Crossland 2009, 2013; Fassin 2011; Fassin and d'Halluin 2007; Fassin and D'halluin 2008; Rosenblatt 2013, 2015; Ticktin 2011). Especially since the 2000s, many scholars observed that there has been a shift of emphasis from "testimony to evidence, from speech to medical data, from the accounts of living people to the testimonies of forensic anthropologists" (Weizman and Herscher 2011, 121) on behalf of bones and bodies. Forensic paradigm has come to dominate how we learn the truth of past violence. Some call this shift the "forensic turn" (Anstett and Dreyfus 2017; Aragüete-Toribio 2022) or the dominance of forensic aesthetics (Keenan and Weizman 2012). This shift was enabled by the "mobilisation of scientific teams, capacity and resources at a global level" (Aragüete-Toribio 2022, 2) especially in cases concerning mass crimes, extrajudicial killings, and enforced disappearances.

The "forensic turn" has often been discussed in relation to places and peoples that experienced excessive and exceptional forms of political violence. Building on these studies that examine the intersections of politics and medicine, specifically the relationship between political violence and forensic medicine in conflict and post-conflict societies, my book zooms into clinical moments when forensic medicine becomes an inseparable aspect of human rights activism while being a routinized bureaucratic practice for state doctors. In other words, departing from the focus on exceptional and necropolitical moments of political violence where the legal framework is suspended, my book explores forensic medical experts who work for the state or human rights organizations and address state violence in police stations, detention centers, prisons, or on the streets in their daily clinical practice. Forensic medical reports are part of the legal and political debate regarding where to draw the distinction between torture as an aberrant practice and legal violence perpetrated by security forces in everyday practices. The prohibition of torture is absolute (*işkence mutlak yasaktır*), meaning that there is no exception to torture (Hajjar 2022). Turkish Criminal Law 5237 at least on paper has perhaps one of the most progressive definitions of torture. It includes psychological harm and does not make a strict separation between torture and ill treatment: "A public officer who performs any act towards a person that is incompatible with human dignity, and which causes that person to suffer physically or mentally, or affects the person's capacity to perceive or his ability to act of his own will or insults them shall be sentenced to a penalty of imprisonment for a term of three to twelve years" (Article 94)[1]. The security forces have the right to use force against the citizens, yet whenever this force is excessive or used "disproportionately," it is considered torture. However, what acts can be labeled as torture is far from being obvious; on the contrary this label requires medical and legal experts to mobilize evidence to make torture visible.

The last sentence of the definition of torture according to the United Nations Convention Against Torture in Article 1 of Part 1 maintains that: "[Torture] does not include pain or suffering arising only from, inherent in, or incidental to lawful sanctions."[2] In the Turkish Penal Code, these lawful sanctions are restricted by the principle of proportionality. "A public official or other persons acting in an official capacity" has control over the use of force, but this force should be applied proportionally. Article 16 of the Law on Duties and Powers of Police (*Polis Vazife ve Salahiyet Kanunu*) regulates the principle of proportionality in Turkish law: "The police are authorized to use force to overcome resistance encountered while performing their duties, to the extent necessary to break this resistance. Within the scope of the authority to use force, physical force, material force, and firearms may be used in a *gradually* increasing manner, depending on the nature and degree of the resistance and in a way that neutralizes those resisting, provided that legal conditions are met."[3] Here the emphasis on *graduation* (as much as proportionality) is crucial because it politically designs an ambiguity regarding what degree of police violence is considered just, legal, and necessary.

The logic of proportionality has significantly reshaped the juridical space in terms of the use of legal force. Eyal Weizman (2012) has been reflecting on the limits and possibilities offered by forensic expertise in detecting human rights violations. According to him, that the use of justifiable levels of violence and of humanitarian/military interventions is allowed in times of emergency constitutes the underlying principle of the present moment. While the 1970s and 1980s are characterized by "testimony on behalf of the victim," the 1990s represent the dominance of political and military force, and the 2000s are characterized by a legalistic strategy, which allows the use of proportional levels of force.

The boundary between acceptable/legitimate and unacceptable/illegitimate forms and levels of violence is constantly made and remade in relation to the inspection and documentation practices of humanitarian doctors and human rights activists. Drawing on the dynamic relationship between the use of alternative clinical evidence and emergent forms of state violence, I argue that as doctors develop complicated forensic techniques to detect torture, not only do the methods of torture change, but the boundaries of the very field of the legitimate use of violence change too. Medicine in general, and forensic medicine in particular, has a special place in the ways we learn about the bodily consequences of violence and whether it can be classified as torture. Rather than producing generalizable knowledge about the world, forensic medical reports produce knowledge about cases, and therefore they are not reproducible and finite (Kruse 2016). Although medical knowledge aims for highest level of generalization for its facts gathered through scientific research, there are limits to the universality of its claims because they are always tested against the body or mind in pain (Harper, Kelly, and Khanna 2015; Scarry 1985). Moreover, each country has a diverse set of legal and administrative frameworks to regulate how medical and forensic facts on state violence are produced and used (Kelly 2015).

Forensic medicine is technology of power that is used to manage populations, create hierarchies of life, or inform legal redress and compensation mechanisms. The promise of forensic medicine to reveal the bodily truth of political violence has been critical for the formation for both progressive and regressive political identities in Turkey. What struck me most during my research on medical documentation of torture and human rights was the question of how those doctors with divergent political positions posit a similar relationship between forensic medical knowledge and the truth of political violence and shared a fantasy regarding the potentially transforming power of forensic truths. Before talking about how this fantasy operates in the context of political violence in Turkey, let me briefly explain how this book engages with the fantasy as an analytical category.

Why Fantasy?

There is a developing literature that approaches fantasy as a precondition of social and historical reality (Rose 1996; Scott 2012) and highlights its role "forging a people's collective and political will" (Glynos 2011a, 66). These scholars have benefited from psychoanalysis' power to interpret irrational, unconscious, and affective dimensions of our politico-social existence and to account for processes and mechanisms that underline the formation of individual and collective subjectivities. The Lacanian theory of fantasy, inspired by the Freudian notion of the split subject, was critical in many of those theories that apply psychoanalysis to account for social and political processes (Glynos and Stavrakakis 2008). Drawing upon Lacan, Žižek politicized the category of fantasy, linking it to debates on ideology, obedience, and domination in modern liberal democracies. For Žižek, ideology does not work through false consciousness but rather through political modes of enjoyment that are established around these ideological fantasies. For a society to claim legitimacy and harmonious evolution, the conflict and antagonism must be repressed through the fantasy structures.

Those who are seeking to understand the conditions of social change (progressive or reactionary, democratic or anti-democratic) have also frequently resorted to psychoanalysis. Because it is not possible to fully understand political projects and identities without fantasy structures that promise to overcome certain obstacles and limitations in current society while at the same time shaping the (desiring) political subject. Rather than seeing fantasy as an illusion or a myth or imagery or unconscious, this book argues that fantasies are structural and logical narratives that inform people's action in linking mundane practices to bigger political ideas and ideologies while at the same time establishing people as ethical subjects. Nationalism and right-wing populism are important venues where phantasmatic narratives dominate the subjects' partial enjoyment in collective practices (Stavrakakis 2020). In a similar vein of thought, it is through these fantasy structures that subjects organize their desire for justice, democracy, and human rights as well as their investment in nationalism, racism, and consumerism (Glynos 2011a). Following Glynos's take on fantasy as an ontological status vis-à-vis the subject, I see fantasy as "a necessary condition for political mobilization and change as much as it is functional to social passivity and maintaining the *status quo*" (Glynos 2011b, 378).

Most crucially for this project, while protecting us from ambiguity and uncertainty, fantasies help form political identities. The category of fantasy thus provides a lens to understanding people's existence within the structures of desire and enjoyment. People "aren't mobilized according to purely objective interests, but rather according to interests created for them by collective fantasies" (Scott 2012, 19). This paradigm proved especially helpful for those who have sought to look beyond the rational and bureaucratic aspects of nation-state in conflict settings and has shown how ethnographic research can contribute to and be inspired from fantasy as analytics. These studies have shown the constitutive role of fantasy in violent processes of state-making (Aretxaga 2001; Feldman 1991; M. T. Taussig 1997;

Aretxaga 2005) and nation-making (Hage 2000; Navaro-Yashin 2002). For example, Aretxaga argued that it is through a world of fantasy "imbued with affect, fear and desire" (Aretxaga 2000, 52) that the state becomes a reality in people's lives. In her examination of counterinsurgency operation in Basque, she demonstrates how the state officials enact terrorist fantasies. When discussing the dynamics of political mobilization in Lebanon, Hermez (2015) makes the observation that politically engaged people see the political world through the lens of cynicism and relate to the state as fantasy. He maintains that people's fantasies of the state give credence to the state's power and existence in Lebanon. Moreover, in many settings state officials and people share a common fantasy. For example, in post-conflict Colombia, legal fantasies about property and the social conflict inform how diverse political actors engage with the transition process and shape future aspirations (Morris 2022).

As I will demonstrate in detail throughout the chapters, pro-state or progressive doctors, politicians, and revolutionaries, as well as victims and perpetrators of political violence articulate their position vis-à-vis violence through forensic fantasies in Turkey. This fantasy about the role of forensic medicine in the cases of political violence has had a dual way of functioning during the last three decades in Turkey. On the one hand, there has been an increase in state-led efforts to centralize, monitor, and facilitate forensic medical knowledge production regarding all acts of violence inflicted by security forces. On the other hand, there has emerged a movement of doctors committed to mobilize their medical expertise for forensic documentation of human rights violations, specifically that of torture. As extensive official and non-official networks and legal regulations on torture documentation have developed, forensic expertise and documents have emerged as a privileged site of truth for state officials, human rights activists, and doctors committed to human rights activism in the last three decades. This multilayered phantasmal investment in the work and power of forensic expertise among doctors in the CFM and doctors in the field of human rights raises two main questions that I address in *Forensic Fantasies*:

Why and how is the Turkish state, which is notorious for its use of extreme forms of violence against its dissident populations, also invested in the denial of violence through the production of forensic documents? How do doctors working in the field of human rights mobilize their own medical expertise against torture, and what are the political and legal consequences of their forensic documentation practices? I situate these questions against the backdrop of political transformations ensuing since the 1980 coup till the present moment in my examination of the parallel and intersecting formations of official and alternative forensic institutions and practices in Turkey in cases of political violence.

There has been a proliferation of ethnographic research on different forms of state violence and their legal, political and social repercussions in Turkey in the last decade. As I discuss in detail in Chapter 1, the 1980 coup d'état is a turning point in the history of political violence in Turkey. While violently repressing the revolutionary and progressive social movements of the 1970s and enabling neoliberal reforms by crushing trade union movements, the coup d'état was also associated with the systematic torture of political inmates.[4] In many incidents of state violence, forensic medicine can be a means of mobilizing ambiguities or avoiding unsettling and inconvenient facts so that consequences of catastrophic or violent events remain knowingly obscure, or as Taussig (1984) would say, remain a "public secret," or as Cohen (2001) would say, remain a "zone of open secrets." Denial of torture through a series of forensic apparatuses, instruments, and epistemologies has emerged as an important performative and constitutive act for the Turkish state since the 1980 coup d'état. One critical incident to this end was the restructuring of the CFM in 1982. Over the years, the CFM's forensic authority had expanded gradually, leaving less space for alternative interpretations of evidence at courts. For example, even when doctors saw bodies that they thought were tortured to death under custody, they would not write that thought down on the grounds that it was the prosecutor's task to make such comments. Epistemological culture of denial at the CFM therefore draws on *aperspectival objectivity*, according to which the reports of the CFM would deny torture without lying or manipulating but rather by promoting a very peculiar understanding of objectivity and presentation of evidence. The format of forensic reports is such that they either discuss other possibilities that might have given rise to a particular scar or wound or refrain from commenting on what might have in fact given rise to a scar or wound. Sustaining a belief in the superiority of facts of violence and reproducing the denial regime vis-à-vis the acts of violence, this epistemology is kept alive by the everyday forensic report-writing practices of doctors at the Council.

The second turning point in the dynamics of political violence came with the foundation of the Kurdistan Workers' Party (Partiya Karkerên Kurdistan, PKK) in 1984. The systematic repression of Kurdish people and the unprecedented level of violence they were subjected to in Diyarbakır Prison after the coup played a central role in the radicalization and growth of the Kurdish political movement throughout the 1980s and 1990s. The state's response was to enforce the State of Emergency Law, which was established by the 1982 Constitution and enacted in 1983, in the eastern and southeastern provinces for a total of fifteen years from 1987 to 2002, with its duration extended forty-six times by parliamentary decision. Those who live under the state of emergency rule were subjected to arbitrary state violence including displacement of populations, enforced disappearances, and extrajudicial killings. It is during those years that torture under police custody and even disappearances under custody became widespread among the members of the radical leftist and Kurdish political groups.[5]

The Kurdish political movement and its transformative impact on the Kurdish population and geography as well as state institutions and state sovereignty throughout the 1990s and afterward have been the topic of several ethnographic research studies in the Kurdish region. Scholars have studied the changing politico-symbolic meaning of the dead for the national identity and sovereignty in the Kurdish conflict and how sovereign violence is inseparable from the state's governmental practices in the region through a dialectical examination of local debt economy (Yoltar 2017; Ozsoy 2010). Despite this bleak picture, the first decade of the 2000s were the years in which state violence began to transform. The acceleration of Turkey's EU accession process in accordance with the PKK's change of policy has created a relatively peaceful political atmosphere. The policy measures to consolidate various democratic reform packages as part of the EU integration process and the intermittent ceasefires declared between the PKK and the Turkish state after the arrest of the PKK leader Abdullah Öcalan in 1999 created a political atmosphere in which brutal forms of state violence (including typical forms of torture such as falanga, which is the beating of the soles of a person's bare foot, or electric shock, that were very widespread throughout the 1980s and 1990s) have become less sustainable for the image of the state at the national and international levels. With their detailed reports on the use of torture in official detention centers and prisons published in 2001, parliamentary Human Rights Violation Investigation Commissions played a crucial role in making torture more visible. In line with these developments, the Justice and Development Party (Adalet ve Kalkınma Partisi, AKP) government announced a "zero tolerance against torture" policy when they came to power in 2002. At the same time, when the state of emergency in the region was totally lifted in 2002, there was an expectation that the perpetrators of these crimes will be put on trial. In the absence of an officially recognized transitional justice mechanism, these efforts remained partial and biased. For example, the state's economic compensation package for the victims of the Kurdish conflict was fraught with injustices and more importantly did not recognize the crimes committed by security forces, suggesting continuity in the state structure (Biner 2020). This period has also produced social movements that sought to put perpetrators on trial for their crimes such as enforced disappearances and torture (Karaman 2016; Aslan 2007; Can 2022). Alongside these grassroots and state-led attempts at transition and reconciliation in cases of extreme forms of state violence that marked the 1980s and 1990s, we have also observed that the scope of state violence in Turkey began to change in the second half of the 2000s.[6] Police stations were equipped with surveillance cameras as stipulated by new laws and regulations in line with the EU harmonization process (Saymaz 2012, 25–44). Furthermore, "classical forms of torture" had also become much less necessary for gathering information because the police were now equipped with highly sophisticated monitoring and surveillance technologies such as bugging and wiretapping technologies.

The changes in forms of state violence have produced studies that explore the intersection of necropolitical violence and governmentality (Bargu 2014a; 2014b) and how the legal and administrative means and procedures were used to discipline oppositional or marginal groups (Yonucu 2018, 2022) or how the biopower and necropower of the state complement each other when it comes to oppressing the Kurdish political movement (Hakyemez 2017; Darıcı and Hakyemez 2022). Even though these studies also mention forensic medical reports, clinical encounters, hospital visits, and autopsy reports when tracing bodily consequences of necropolitical violence, these elements are not at the heart of their research. *Forensic Fantasies* undertakes a multilayered analysis of medicine vis-à-vis violence to understand how tortured bodies can be objects of necropolitical violence, biopolitical care, and scientific expertise through medicine.

Medicine can be used to violate the body (Agamben 1998) or to facilitate the work of torturers (Wilcox 2011), or alternatively it can help the tortured heal. Indeed, the encounters between tortured bodies and medical professionals are always fraught with the tension between necropolitics and biopolitics, between violation of the body and care for the body (Bargu 2016; Can 2019; Kelly 2012; Puar 2017). Doctors in this book engage in a struggle around the body and bodily evidence in the aftermath of violence, pushing us to rethink the vicissitudes of forensic documentation in relation to political violence. However, not all doctors are examining the body to find forensic traces of violence. Occupying positions as diverse as state officials, human rights practitioners, and official expert witnesses, these doctors can make torture and ill treatment either legible or illegible through forensic documentation depending on what extent their expert identities are shaped by forensic fantasies.

I deploy the term *forensic fantasy* as a critical lens to describe how forensic doctors occupying diverse ideological and professional positions develop different degrees of attachment to their communities and professions vis-à-vis the stories of forensic documentation and its potential consequences in terms of restricting, eliminating, or denying state violence. There has been a common understanding around the ultimate superiority of scientific objectivity when addressing the consequences of state violence and that it can be addressed only through scientific methods, as if the boundary between the legal and illegal, formal and informal, can be drawn with the help of forensic medicine. How are we to understand this shared fantasy of scientific objectivity in addressing the consequences of violence in the context of Turkey? This book shows how these fantasies are daily sustained through alliances and tensions between doctors and the victims of torture, their political organization, state authorities in clinical settings where intimate communities are critical to the vernacularization of human rights, and the moderation and restriction of state violence that is built in the absence of reconciliatory mechanisms to reckon with it. It is through the contentions and alliances within these social and political networks that one can talk about the efficacy or inefficacy of the truth of state violence.

Forensic Fantasies pursues three central arguments: First, forensic documentation works through fantasy—namely that medical witnessing of violence produces scientific and objective truth, puts an end to undue state violence, and performs justice. This fantasy animates doctors' affective relationship with their expert identities, patients, and human rights politics. It illustrates how expert identity and expert communities are founded through fantasy. Second, as forensic documents travel between institutions, families, and human rights organizations as the objects of desire needed by legal processes and convincing political demands, they shape the political imagination of oppositional groups and orient them toward a politics of truth as the strategy for challenging state authority.

Rather than opposing facts and fantasies or truths and emotions, the book suggests that finding facts about human rights violations is a fantasy-induced political project, and thus forensic fantasies have in fact founded the field of human rights in Turkey as the politics of veracity. Third, to the extent that the trajectories of state violence and human rights politics coalesce around the logic of proof and denial, human rights politics and post-violence justice mechanisms prove ineffective as long as they revolve around the economy of evidence in the age of post-truth politics, especially because states are extremely equipped to invest in and boost this economy of evidence.

These arguments are based on my research with doctors specializing in torture documentation and archival research on forensic documents of torture in Turkey. I primarily focus on encounters between doctors and victims of state violence at the CFM (official authority), public hospitals (primary site for mandatory medical examination of detainees), and the Human Rights Foundation of Turkey (a nongovernmental organization specializing in torture documentation). Doctors in these settings play key roles in diagnosing suffering and injustice that people experience under the state's care. These clinical encounters are unique in that these doctors are often the firsthand witnesses of the bodily suffering of these individuals, who stand in front of them as patients first and foremost as opposed to other legal or political labels attributed to them such as detainees, criminals, terrorists, or political activists. Throughout my research, I wanted to understand how doctors developed diverse ways of observing, analyzing, and reporting the consequences of police violence in different clinical settings. I conducted twenty-four months of multi-sited ethnographic research (2011–2013) and eight months of follow-up research (2018 and 2019) in public hospitals, the Human Rights Foundation of Turkey, and the Turkish Medical Association. In total I conducted fifty-five interviews with doctors who work in these institutions and who produce medico-legal reports in these different clinical settings. I regularly visited the Istanbul branch of the Human Rights Foundation of Turkey, but I also visited its Ankara, Diyarbakır, and İzmir branches over the course of my research. I wanted to understand the history and workings of this foundation, as well as how doctors in the foundation have kept their relationship with the people and groups that are more likely to experience police violence. Medical forensic reports are mandatory in Turkey before and after detention, and in order to understand how these routinized medical reports for detainees are prepared, I visited public hospitals and their forensics and emergency departments where doctors are tasked with preparation of forensic medical reports for bureaucratic and legal purposes. Finally, I could not secure permission to conduct research in the CFM, but I mobilized personal connections to reach out to the doctors who have worked and are still working in the Council. I often met with the doctors outside their workplace. Some doctors invited me to their offices, and I was also able to make short observations either in their offices or waiting halls, which were outside the Council building. I conducted interviews with fifteen forensic doctors who were either still working or used to work at the Council. Whenever I was able to get close to the clinical spaces where medical examinations took place, I made observations regarding institutional infrastructures and materiality of documents to understand how examination rooms, handcuffs, physical infrastructure, and official forms inform report-writing processes as well as circulation of forensic documents. Such an approach enabled me to demonstrate that these fantasies are maintained within and through the material infrastructures of bureaucracies and human rights organizations as well as solidarity networks among doctors. I also deployed archival research (in the archives of the Human Rights Association and the Human Rights Foundation of Turkey) and media research (in the newspapers of *Cumhuriyet* and *Hürriyet*) to draw a genealogical analysis of how the epistemological categories of torture, documents, evidence, suffering, pain, human rights, and humanitarianism have traveled through time in Turkey's recent political history. Finally, conducting follow-up research for the book in 2018 and 2019 allowed me to see the changes and continuities in forms of state violence in the country from the perspective of doctors who encounter the victims of state violence regularly.

Conducting research in a period that covers almost a decade allowed me to observe how an increasingly authoritarian atmosphere in the country transformed research dynamics. My research just ended when the Gezi resistance erupted and was repressed in 2013. It was the first popular uprising against the increasingly authoritarian rule of the AKP government since it came to power in 2002 (Yörük and Yüksel 2014). The Gezi protests were followed by the collapse of peace negotiations between the Turkish state and the PKK in 2015, and finally, the 2016 coup attempt by the Gülen movement. All these events further normalized and facilitated the suppression and criminalization of dissenting groups including students, politicians, journalists, and academics. When I resumed my field research to conduct follow-up interviews with doctors in public hospitals and human rights organizations in 2018, the political atmosphere in the country was very different from the early 2010s (Saluk 2024; Can 2020). I was surprised to realize that most research participants were reluctant to reveal personal knowledge about themselves, and many of them did not allow me to turn on my recorder during the interview. Overall, my feeling was that people were more suspicious and careful about what they were saying about state violence and their work as doctors. Their attitude reflected the increasingly repressive political atmosphere in the country. Throughout the book I anonymized all names except for Şebnem Korur Fincancı, who has been the vocal spokesperson of this movement many times in different capacities since the 1990s. Most of the events she participated in and I followed during my research were in the public domain.

The book is divided into two parts. The first part consists of three chapters that examine how the fantasy about the power of forensic documentation and evidence operates in criminal law and in various institutions such as the CFM, the Human Rights Foundation of Turkey, and public hospitals where doctors have been producing documents of police violence over the last three decades. These chapters show how the fantasy about documentation animates doctors' relations with their patients, their expert work, and the principles of medical ethics through the historical and ethnographic analysis of clinical encounters in these settings. Moving beyond dualistic debates on whether facts and truths are constructed or waiting to be discovered, the first part of the book demonstrates how collective fantasies about the power of forensic truths keep doctors committed to either searching for violence or erasing its traces. In the second part of the book, I explore how forensic fantasies transform political subjectivities and imaginations of doctors and dissident groups in Turkey in the last three decades. To this end, I focus on two critical events that concern political mobilization through forensic documentation. One is about ill prisoners who need forensic documentation of their illness for their release, and the second concerns condemning state violence by documenting its violence on the bodies after the Gezi uprising.

Outline

The first chapter examines the reorganization of the CFM following the 1980s coup d'état, highlighting its role in establishing a regime of denial through forensic medical practices. Focusing some key figures and incidents in the history of the Council, I trace how forensic fantasy has operated as part and parcel of the denial regime. The doctors working for this institution had sophisticated and critical insights about the limitations of their jobs and the problems of hegemonic forensic epistemology that informed their practices at the Council. Although there were doctors who consciously manipulated the findings of violence, most doctors did not deny violence purposefully. On the contrary, these doctors had a peculiar relationship with facts that didn't simply construct a denial regime; they were trained to register and record the "facts" of violence while disregarding the contextual information or inference. Doctors' phantasmal investment in medical veracity enabled an ambivalent role for medicine in the sense that the Council ended up producing detailed forensic reports and medical facts about political violence that would later be remobilized as proofs of torture. This argument allows for avoiding a reductive understanding of the relationship between medicine and violence by showing the more subtle ways in which medicine could become both complicit with and antidote to torture through the deployment of a neutral and objective medical stance at the same time.

The second chapter deals with doctors' efforts to document torture against the backdrop of the centralization of official expert knowledge production and the consolidation of a regime of denial throughout the 1980s. At the heart of my inquiry lies a group of progressive, leftist, or humanist forensic doctors who have mobilized their medical expertise and solidarity networks to provide medical care and documentation for those who were subjected to torture in prison or in a police station. While they prepared counter or alternative forensic documents that contest the claims of official medical documents, it was forensic fantasies that informed and inspired their communal and individual subjectivities. Analyzing historical and ethnographic data about torture documentation in Turkey since the 1980 coup d'état, I discuss the limits and possibilities of radical documentation practices as a political project, showing how doctors' politicized forensic fantasies draw upon the state's power to recognize them as documents of violence. Chapter 2 demonstrates that the proof and fantasy of human rights violations are inseparable as both are dialectically linked to forms of state violence through the fantasies about the forensic documentation of violence and its power to end torture in the country. I argue that the doctors' investment in forensic fantasies makes us forget historical and political dynamics other than forensic documents and documentation such as the encounters with the torture victims and responses of state officials that keep forensic fantasies alive in the first place.

As early as mid-1990s, doctors' determination to document torture was reciprocated by the then government's decision to introduce a progressive anti-torture regulation about detainees' access to health and medical examination that required all detainees be examined by a doctor before and after detention. This two-part medical-examination mechanism aimed to ensure that any police brutality under custody did not go undocumented. The third chapter examines routinized encounters between the police and doctors through the physical examination of the detainee and how doctors, who were invested in collecting facts about the body, would devote themselves to creating ideal examination environments and examining the detainees thoroughly. Chapter 3 further shows that this devotion would be possible only if doctors employed by state hospitals were embedded in other political networks that kept them motivated in undertaking the challenging task of making torture visible with documents. It also demonstrates that despite the power and good intentions of these networks, producing the "good documents" that "proved" torture as required by the state inevitably reproduced legal fetishism and the idea of the state as a unified entity.

Forensic documents traveling between institutions, families, and human rights organizations have shaped the political imagination of doctors, oppositional groups, prisoners, their supporters, and human rights activists orienting them toward a politics of truth based on forensic documents as the strategy for challenging state authority. Chapter 4 examines the unintended political consequences of the extensive use of forensic documents in cases concerning prisoners' health in the last two decades. I analyze two critical events concerning prisoners' health in Turkey, namely the release of hundreds of hunger strikers beginning in 2001, and the release of sick prisoner Güler Zere in 2010 on medical humanitarian grounds with the help of forensic documents issued by the CFM. I discuss how these critical incidents transformed how political activists and human rights activists engaged with the problems within the prison system, specifically how the political and legal demands regarding the health of prisoners were increasingly mediated through forensic documents prepared by doctors and submitted not only to the court but also to diverse publics. This chapter explores how the suffering bodies of the imprisoned people become an object of contention among various medical-expert witnessing practices at the CFM, university hospitals, and state hospitals. Discussing how diverse forensic documents are mobilized while making legal and political claims regarding the health of the imprisoned, this chapter argues that forensic fantasies have captivated the political imaginations not only of certain doctors or state officials but also prisoners, their supporters, and human rights activists.

Doctors and their investment in documents are the subject topic of Chapter 5. In this chapter, I draw on the Gezi protests in summer 2013 as well as on my observations in makeshift clinics during protests and at meetings and conferences where doctors addressed the health-related consequences of police violence, especially the use of tear gas and pepper spray. I show that pro–human rights doctors developed a fragmented perception of the protest as they were committed to finding ways of documenting disproportionate use of police violence. Their desire to forensically document violence moved doctors' focus from a collective political action to what was done to the protestors. In other words, their view of political bodies was restricted to bodies that were in pain. At the same time, as they sought to provide medical care to those who suffered and help them document their scars, these doctors found themselves in the middle of the protests. Since they were physically closer to the protestors and their expert witnessing produced evidence of state violence, their bodies were also subjected to police violence. Their actions were criminalized, and some doctors were even put on trial. These doctors used forensic fantasy and depended on documents as a form of collective resistance both during the protests and in their aftermath while they defended themselves in the court.

This book starts with the observation that forensic documents have gained unprecedented importance for human rights projects in Turkey and argues that documents are appealing to those who have to globally fight denial regimes everywhere because these documents are a "truth-claim-making machine" (Keenan and Steyerl 2014, 62). This is even more so for forensic documents that harness scientific and medical-expert knowledge in detecting bodily harms inflicted by state officials and bodily illnesses that occur under the state care. Moreover, forensic documents as a truth-making-machine compels a response, and it is the belief in this response that has kept doctors in the human rights field and torture documentation in Turkey. State authorities have indeed over the years designed anti-torture regulations such as a mandatory health examination of a detainee, moderation of torture methods, and wider uses of medical humanitarian clauses through forensic documents in cases of ill prisoners.

Today the response seems to be withering. In the context of the global rise of the right-wing populist movement, state officials of the increasingly authoritarian government have become less interested in denying these violations; instead, they let them turn into spectacles and never-ending public debates, which ultimately leads to political apathy. Medical examination of detainees does not prevent police brutality even when it is proven with forensic documents. Seriously ill prisoners are not released even if they have documents required by the state for their release. Citizens and especially activists are increasingly disillusioned by the power of scientific documents in restricting state violence and receiving a meaningful response. I therefore theorize *forensic fantasies* as an increasingly deteriorating ground upon which the belief in the superiority of facts is built, even though doctors fighting for human rights in Turkey still hold onto it as something that inspires their communal and political sociality. Overall, this book demonstrates that the limits of truth in cases of violence depend on the fantasies about forensic evidence materialized in clinical encounters, social relations, state bureaucracies, and legal regulations. Despite the critiques of transitional justice or reconciliatory mechanisms and their reliance on legal structures in the 1990s, there was an overarching consensus on the importance of finding the truth about the past state crimes and the truth that could lead to a more peaceful future. The peacebuilding projects no longer enjoy their previous popularity, and nation states are less willing to face the crimes they were accused of. Even if forensic fantasies are less and less effective in restricting violence, they continue to inspire alternative communities and radical subjectivities of doctors as specific intellectuals that can intervene in the hegemonic regime of truth production. The book thus shows the world-making and community-building power of truth for those who cherish fantasies about its power.

CHAPTER 1

======

Phantasmal Commitment to Veracity

A group of forensic doctors from Turkey was asked to join the international forensic team for mass-grave exhumations in Bosnia in 1996. Dr. Ahmet, who was back then working in the CFM, was part of this group. For over two weeks, he attended exhumations, conducted autopsies, and wrote forensic reports. One year later, a team of international judges visited Turkey and interviewed Dr. Ahmet and other doctors who attended these exhumations in Bosnia. The international judges wanted to find out whether the Turkish doctors had any material evidence about whether these exhumed bodies in Bosnia were not in fact murdered because almost all doctors from Turkey in the international exhumation team had avoided listing any causes of death when filling out the commentary sections of the forensic reports. Indeed, Dr. Ahmet refrained from expressing an opinion and making a commentary as to why and how the death might have occurred by not filling out the last section of the forensic reports. Only after this incident did Dr. Ahmet start to realize that there was something peculiar with the report-writing tradition in Turkey. During our interview, he retrospectively thought about what he saw in Bosnia: "People might have been put in mass graves during war due to many reasons such as contagious diseases, or absence of conditions for proper burial. But in mass graves in the Tuzla area where we worked the situation was different. Due to the nature of the soil, the bodies and clothes were kept relatively intact." Dr. Ahmet could see that people in the mass grave were all blindfolded and their hands were tied behind them. This was homicide, and there was no other option, he added. However, back then, Dr. Ahmet did not write this in the report because he thought that this was not a scientific observation. For him, it was not the responsibility of doctors but of the judges or prosecutors to make such commentaries because doctors' work, he believed, should remain within scientific boundaries. This is what he was taught at medical school, and this is how he practiced forensic medicine at the CFM (i.e., the ultimate official authority on expert documents). This chapter examines the forensic fantasies that inform the formation and consolidation of this type of forensic report-writing culture after the 1980 coup d'état and its consequences for understanding, restricting, and reproducing political violence.

The 1980 coup d'état is considered a turning point in the history of Turkey, as it not only paved the way for the rapid neoliberal transformation of the economy and social relations but also violently repressed the strong leftist movements of the 1970s. The extreme forms of military violence experienced by political inmates, especially leftist revolutionary groups and Kurdish people, have had long-term consequences for the political atmosphere of the country. It is estimated that 650,000 people were arrested after the coup. A total of 230,000 people were judged in 210,000 lawsuits, 7,000 people were given the death penalty, 517 persons were sentenced to death, and 50 of those given the death penalty were executed. Three hundred people died suspiciously. It was also documented that 171 people died because of torture. Despite the severity of the political violence inflicted on dissident groups, it was also clear that these groups were not killed or disappeared en masse. Rather, the military government undertook mass arrests, heavily tortured political dissidents and ethnic minorities in police stations, military barracks, and prisons, and then, after a while, released them back into society. This approach operated as a governmental strategy to repress the opposition through a political atmosphere of fear and uncertainty via injured bodies. The political consequences of this violence have been unprecedented in the country as systematic violence against Kurdish people in prisons has facilitated the emergence of the Kurdish guerrilla movement in the southeastern part of Anatolia. Stories of torture resistance have been told in memoirs, political debates, and personal narratives in ways to shape individual and collective political identities of leftists in the last three decades. However, the instrumental role medicine has played in this brutal history of political violence has remained covert and understudied.

The junta made the detainees (the so-called opponents of the regime) undergo a series of bureaucratic and legal mechanisms through which they kept detailed records and gathered intelligence. Some doctors participated in torture sessions, some doctors used their medical knowledge to surveil and control dissident groups through medical experiments, and some doctors refused to provide medical care and treatment for ill or injured prisoners or detainees when the latter went through several official medical institutions for examination, treatment, or documentation (Soyer 1993, 68–72; 1996, 73–127). Medical practices and medical documents have emerged as a privileged technology of power for the post-coup regime and the following governments in their interactions with the so-called dissident people.

It was at the height of the military regime in 1982 that the junta decided to restructure the CFM, which then became the ultimate official expert institution to produce forensic knowledge on all suspicious cases including the violence inflicted by security forces. This restructuring mainly meant the centralization of a diverse range of forensic practices under the roof of the CFM and its branches that are dispersed across Turkey. It was CFM and its institutional workings that produced a division of labor between science and law, between the clinical and the legal, which would in turn inform forensic report-writing practices of doctors in Turkey, specifically how doctors interpreted and documented consequences of state violence. These forensic documents often would render invisible the acts of violence by registering only the biological and physical consequences on the body, leaving aside the broader social and political context within which acts of violence took place.

Was that all there was, though? Was CFM just an instrument to erase and normalize state violence? On the one hand, as critical scholars and political activists in Turkey suggest, the military and post-military governments did rely on forensic documents to maintain their legitimacy as these documents helped them deny the traces of state violence. As Dr. Ahmet's story at the beginning of this chapter shows, denial is intrinsic to this forensic culture and operation of the CFM because of assumptions regarding the boundaries between law, medicine, and violence and hence assumptions regarding epistemology. This epistemology is kept alive by in the everyday forensic report-writing practices of doctors at the Council. But on the other hand, it was not just the state that exploited the meticulous reports written by doctors at the CFM. The detailed factual accounts about the tortured, injured, and dead bodies were used for counter-purposes such as the documentation of torture. How can we then account for this dual role of the official medical knowledge and practice during and after the systematic state violence? More specifically, how can we understand the role of forensic medicine during the times of systematic state violence in terms of justifying, undermining, or challenging the consequences of it?

Drawing upon the interviews with forensic doctors who worked in the Council as well as forensic reports prepared by the Council, as well as popular and expert opinions about the Council's contentious report-writing practices, I demonstrate that the unwritten rules, conventions, and tendencies at the Council not only enabled the state to erase violence but also created the habitus through which doctors, with their fantasies invested in forensic veracity, learned and internalized the notion of scientific suspicion. This particular kind of training culture that praised scientific suspicion as a path to objective truth also brought about a phantasmal commitment to medical facts about the body and making them oblivious to the broader sociological or political context within which political violence took place. Specifically, whenever doctors are asked to write forensic reports on ill or injured bodies or prepare autopsy report after examining a deceased person, they mostly work in accordance with specific rules and procedures that keep them connected to medical facts. Except for extreme cases where explicitly pro-state doctors consciously manipulate the facts of violence, there is always some connection to the medical truth of violence in these reports. That is how an institution originally turned into a productive space to prove what it was initially designed to deny.

In this chapter, I first show how the military regime instrumentalized medicine to control and rule over the bodies of political prisoners immediately after the coup. This occurred during the years (especially between 1980 and 1990) when many doctors were accused of participating in torture sessions, conducting unethical experiments on prisoners, or refusing to provide treatment for prisoners or detainees either out of ideological hostility or fear of retaliation from security forces. However, besides these extreme cases of direct and open collaboration between doctors and security forces, there are other encounters between political bodies and medical apparatuses that necessitate more subtle analyses of medicine's complicity in violence. Then, I examine doctors' report-writing practices at the CFM and argue that doctors' phantasmal commitment to forensic veracity has been ambivalently productive. Meanwhile the official doctors in this Council established a regime of denial by preparing forensic reports that reproduced the strict division between science and law, the clinical and the legal. However, their investment in the former, namely their phantasmal commitment to forensic veracity and scientific suspicion, enabled human rights activists, doctors, and lawyers to use these same documents as proof of state violence in coming years.

Medicine as a Technology of Repressive Biopower: The Complicit Doctors and the Unethical Experiments on the "State Enemies"

In the aftermath of the coup d'état, when political activists were arrested en masse, the military junta saw this as an opportunity to "understand" and "correct" these "terrorists" and "anarchists" (Bekaroğlu 2010; Dindar 2010; Mavioğlu 2004). The plan was to allow pro-state, ultranationalist, or conservative doctors to conduct clinical experiments and research, which would in turn give clues regarding how to cure anarchism and radicalism. The testimony of a renowned psychiatrist and right-wing politician Mehmet Bekaroğlu in military prisons confirms how the state's medical ideology to "fix" dissidents worked in practice. After being appointed as a psychiatrist at Metris Prison, one of the most notorious military prisons of the time hosting political prisoners, the military administration of the prison asked Bekaroğlu in 1983 to "treat communism" and "correct" "patients/deviants." According to Bekaroğlu, this project failed because the state authorities lacked the complexity to comprehend those engaged in political activism. Of his experience at Metris Prison, Bekaroğlu said this in an interview (Mavioğlu 2004):

> I knew why I was appointed there. I was told: "you are a psychiatrist. You know what passes in their minds. Hypnotize them." This was their favorite word. They wanted me to dissuade political prisoners from going on hunger strikes[1] by using hypnosis. There was one prisoner who was on hunger strike I can't forget. The hospital did not accept him, so he was brought to the infirmary. They wanted to drip-feed him, but as soon as he woke up, he had removed the serum. The commanders got angry with me and told me to hypnotize him, to make him sleep so that he would not resist the treatment. . . . They had hoped that I would do anything they wanted to the leftist prisoners since I was a right-wing person.

Because Bekaroğlu didn't comply with their orders, they began to call him "the right winger who doesn't collaborate." He was not the only medical doctor approached by the military immediately after the 1980 coup d'état. The government even set up a team of experts that sought to examine the psychology of political prisoners to come up with proper medical treatment to "fix" them. As Bekaroğlu (2010) would report: "Under the name of the rehabilitation of political prisoners, these so-called professors and 'scientists,' such as Dr. Turan Itil and Dr. Ayhan Songar,[2] sought to develop methods that will 'remove' the personalities and thoughts of the prisoners. They therefore deserved to be called the fathers of torture in prison."

To medicalize and regulate political activism, these people conducted a series of conferences, experiments, and research. Under the guise of being psychiatrists, they engaged in practices of indoctrination as part of psychological warfare. They did experiments against human dignity and tried various drugs on prisoners, using them as guinea pigs. One complicit institution for these purposes was the Hafize Zekeriya Itil Foundation (HZI), which was founded by Dr. Turan Itil in 1971 and named after his mother and father, to conduct research in neuropsychiatry. Following the coup d'état in 1980, the HZI's main field of research became "the medical and sociological analysis of the anarchic events of the pre-September 12 period" (Dindar 2010, 30). In the words of his sister Muazzez Ilmiye Çığ, Turan Itil, wanted to do something for the country after the September 12 coup and contacted the junta. He wanted to do research on how the youth get involved in "terrorist activities," and that's how he decided to return to Turkey from the United States.[3] HZI specialized in neuropsychiatry and conducted experiments on political prisoners up until 1990 in collaboration with state institutions. Dr. Itil conducted experiments on approximately 5,000 people, 2,700 of them prisoners (Şahin 2010, 8). There is still no comprehensive research on the scope of the activities carried out by the HZI. We know from the former prisoners' testimonies that prison administrations permitted hundreds of political prisoners to be taken to the offices of the HZI. These prisoners were not informed about the content of the experiments before being submitted to them.

In 2010, the AKP government held a referendum to gain approval for a constitutional amendment package. As a result, Article 15, which prevented the trial of those who were involved in September 12 coup d'état, was removed from the Constitution. Shortly after, the victims of the coup started to file criminal complaints. Those who were used as guinea pigs in these experiments began to share

their experiences and filed official complaints against the doctors
and psychiatrists who took part in these experiments and misused
their medical privilege to intervene in their bodily and psychological integrity. For example, Recep Küçükıssız, who was sentenced to
life imprisonment two times for involvement in right-wing political activism and lived abroad for almost a decade before returning
the country, recognized Dr. Turan Itil on television. He remembers
seeing him in a white uniform in Mamak Prison asking weird questions and filling out prisoners' forms. After Itil's visit, he says, things
changed for worse in the prison.[4] Consider the statements of Mehmet, a political prisoner imprisoned after the coup. In his testimony,
Mehmet explains what he experienced upon being taken from the
prison without his consent right before the 1983 hunger strike:

> There was too much pressure in Metris Prison. One day
> they gathered 10 of us in the prison yard. All of us had
> received heavy sentences but were members of different
> political groups. They put us in a military vehicle and
> brought us to a five-story building. When we entered, we
> saw other people in prison uniforms. I asked them where
> they came from. They came from different cities. Most of
> them were ordinary prisoners. They took us to the fifth
> floor. Everything was very clean and luxurious. They had
> prepared that floor for us. . . . We insisted upon seeing a
> person in charge and someone came. He said, "you were
> brought here by permission of the judicial advisory." Then
> we asked to see this document. Then another person came
> in and said, "you were brought here upon a decision made
> by the military court." Then we wanted to see that written
> order. (Quoted from Dindar 2010, 30)

When the group insisted on seeing the written order, the infamous
psychiatrist Dr. Ayhan Songar came in. Dr. Songar was the founder
of the department of psychiatry at Cerrahpaşa Medical School—one
of Turkey's best medical schools—and known for ultranationalist

and conservative worldviews. Different from the previous persons, he did not stand at the door but directly entered the room. He said to them, "You are here for research conducted by the university" (Dindar 2010, 30). Then he went on to explain how this research was independent and how the results of this research would be used for the prisoners' benefit. At first, he said that the group was going to stay for a week. However, when the prisoners refused to stay or talk, he wanted to convince them to talk for five to ten minutes just for the research. But they didn't accept that offer either. The evening of that day the prisoners were taken back to the prison.

Dr. Songar presented the results of this research at a conference in 1984, which forensic scientists, psychiatrists, and social workers attended (Songar 1984) and aimed to explore the personal and social roots of the deviant behavior and mental features of "terrorists" (Gürbilek 1993). An article written by Sayari titled "The Terrorist Movement in Turkey: Social Composition and Generational Changes" published in *Conflict Quarterly* refers to the findings of the research conducted by Dr. Itil as follows: "The partial findings of a major personality and psychometric examination of the imprisoned terrorists similarly underscore the very low cultural and educational level of the followers. According to this study, the majority of these young people have low IQs, some display symptoms of minimal brain dysfunction, and most are subject to 'herd psychology'" (Sayari 1987, 28). In 1984, the practices of the HZI were made public for the first time in an issue of *Nokta Magazine*. Dr. Itil gave an interview for the *Nokta Magazine* where he discussed how he and other psychiatrists interviewed terrorists in different prisons in Turkey for this international research and further elaborated on how there was no suspicion as to who was a terrorist and who was not. For him, time was a productive means of "correction": "We worked on individuals who really did commit a crime. . . . But the best medicine is age. No one over 40 becomes a terrorist. They have to be kept imprisoned till they are 40. This is an expensive method but better than execution" (Şahin 2010, 8).

Upon *Nokta*'s expositions, the Ministry of Health as well as the Istanbul Public Prosecutors Office initiated investigations of the allegations as to the use of humans as guinea pigs in experiments in the same year. However, the investigation halted on the grounds that there is no regulation against such unethical experiments. The office of the HZI stayed open until 1990, when an illegal radical leftist party bombed it. After entering the office with guns, the militants said: "We are revolutionaries. We will not harm you. We are here for Turan Itil. Now we are going to place a bomb upstairs. After we leave, close your ears and lie down" (*Milliyet Daily*, June 22, 1990). The revolutionary militants also left a leaflet in the office that said: "The HZI foundation works for American drug monopolies and is financed by the CIA, and it was destroyed by us." After this event, Dr. Itil left the country, and all the activities of the HZI ended.

The HZI experience is an early and radical example of how the state officials could use medicine for political purposes through experiments on the bodies of political prisoners. The fact that the HZI, which itself was physically located very close to a police station in Gayrettepe that was notorious for torture practices at the time, could operate for almost two decades at the height of political mobilization confirms the state's support for this type of intervention into the bodies of political prisoners or ignorance of and indifference to such intervention at the very least. There were also stories about doctors who refused to provide proper medical examination or treatment when political prisoners were transferred from the prison or the police station to a hospital for medical reasons. Political prisoners also had testimonies about how some doctors worked in collaboration with police officers in police stations during torture sessions. These doctors were reported to have medically treated the tortured prisoners so that the police could further exercise torture (Soyer 1993, 1996). The events surrounding the HZI experiments as well as the testimonies of political prisoners regarding doctors' complicity in torture increased sensitivity of doctors' professional association to questions of medical ethics and doctors' complicity in violence. Beginning in the mid-1980s, the Turkish Medical Association released statements condemning doctors who are engaged in such acts and wrote petitions to the Ministry of Justice inquiring about these doctors who are said to have participated in torture sessions or refused to provide proper health care for detainees and prisoners on ideological grounds or for fear of retaliation from the security forces (Soyer 1996, 116).[5]

The experiments on prisoners were unethical and aimed to control and regulate "unruly" behavior of political militants. These are extreme cases illustrating how the bodies of political prisoners were medically targeted or neglected on ideological grounds. However, the use of medicine for political purposes was taking place within the broader context of denial where medical institutions were working to undermine the health consequences of state violence. Doctors who conducted these experiments were not deviant figures. Rather, they were respected professors. They had prestige, authority, and connections. For example, Dr. Ayhan Songar worked at the CFM both before and after the coup. Such radical and ideologically invested figures could find a legitimate space for themselves in official expert settings. However, what is more interesting is that most doctors who were working in the state's official expert institution, namely the CFM, were not necessarily politically or ideologically invested in the system. On the contrary, many of them were ordinary experts minding their own business and practicing their profession to the best of their ability and preparing forensic reports. Yet, the ways in which the CFM was structured enabled the systematic denial of violence at the institutional level regardless of intentions of its employee doctors. Most of these forensic documents as the artifacts of expert witnessing had an ambivalent status in terms of their relationship to the facts of violence due to the phantasmal investment in the politics of veracity cultivated in the training culture of the Council.

Reproducing the Denial Regime via Forensic Reports

Due to its capacity to perform scientific investigation of bodily remains and forensic autopsies for legal purposes, the CFM is the premier authority on investigation and documentation of unnatural deaths and various sorts of crimes. The expert reports prepared by other scientific institutions like forensic medicine departments in universities or by private doctors can easily be declared null and void in the face of CFM reports by the higher courts. Therefore, heads of courts would have to turn to the Council for scientific expert reports, especially when they need expert opinion during trials.

Historical research on CFM takes one directly to a single name: Dr. Şemsi Gök (1921–2002). As the head of the Council during the 1980-coup, Dr. Gök was tasked with rewriting the CFM law in 1982. Dr. Gök's restructuring of the Council reveals the contradictions surrounding forensic medicine in terms of naming, addressing, and diagnosing political violence in the country and therefore provides important insights regarding the relationship between violence and medicine. In his work, Dr. Gök introduced six departments (biology, morgue, chemistry, physics, traffic, observation) specializing in research and six councils specializing in report-writing. With the new regulation, he aimed to replace personal relationships within the CFM with that of a bureaucratic structure based on commissions and councils while maintaining the hierarchical relationship between forensic medicine and judiciary. Indeed, there has always been very close relations between the highest cadres of the judiciary system and the professors of forensic medicine. Beginning from the first National Forensic Medicine Days organized in 1982, such organizations as the CFM brought together members of the Supreme Court, prosecutors, judges and forensic experts (Gök 1985). Many forensic doctors I interviewed describe these symposia as highly bureaucratic and serious events that involved top cadres of judiciary. The primary mission of the Council has remained the same, serving justice for over a century. The CFM is affiliated with the Ministry of Justice but not the Ministry of Health, even though the majority of its employees are doctors. Forensic tasks were conducted under the Ministry of Health up until the early twentieth century. This changed in 1917 before the republic came into being and before the CFM was attached to the Ministry of Justice. Forensic medicine law changed three times during the republic, first in 1926 (Law no. 813), then in

1953 (Law no. 6119), and finally in 1982 (Law no. 2659), yet none of the laws changed its affiliation with the Ministry of Justice. Doctors who are working in the field of human rights argue that the fact that this Council is directly subordinate to the Ministry of Justice renders it structurally vulnerable to political manipulation. Election bulletins of almost all political parties have an article that promises to guarantee the independence of the CFM, yet no government has changed its main organizational structure since 1982.[6]

Known as the founding figure of modern forensic medicine in Turkey, Dr. Gök was a professor of pathology and trained generations of forensic doctors beginning in the 1960s and ending in the late 1980s at the CFM and the forensic medicine department at Cerrahpaşa Medical School. He had the scientific expertise and experience in conducting autopsies and determining causes of death. It was nobody other than him who wrote the first books on forensic medicine in Turkish. He was also teaching forensic medicine at the Cerrahpaşa Medical School when he was assigned as the head of the CFM in 1969. During his tenure, Dr. Gök gradually increased its sphere of influence. He was able to gather all well-known and important professors of medicine under the Council while establishing good relations with members of the judiciary and other state officials. He even moved the CFM to the university campus in Cerrahpaşa in order to facilitate scientific collaboration between the forensic medicine department at the medical school and the CFM.

Dr. Gök had to resign from his position as the head of CFM a year later because of a change in the law that prevented a state official from being simultaneously appointed to two official institutions. Yet, this did not prevent him from increasing his sphere of influence in the field of forensic medicine during these years. When the law changed again in 1977, he was brought back as the head of the Council, where he remained until his retirement in 1987. For almost a decade, he was both the head of the CFM and the head of the Forensic Medicine Department at Cerrahpaşa Medical School (Gök and Özen 1982). Most of the forensic doctors I interviewed knew Dr. Gök personally. Some had even taken classes from him when they were at the medical school and later worked under him at the CFM. The younger ones remember how he frequently visited the Council even after his retirement. All narratives about him describe him as a dominant and God-like person.

Dr. Ahmet, with whom I opened this chapter, is now a middle-aged forensic medicine expert and works as an associated professor at the forensic medicine department in a public university. When he was doing his internship there, Dr. Gök was still working at the Council. He tells his experience of working as an intern at the Council under the tutelage of Dr. Gök in the following way: "There was him then. He was the head of the Institution. He was the only decision maker. He was everything. Nobody could say a thing against him. He had charm. You had to keep a distance between yourself and him. If you didn't, you would immediately kiss his hands. You would try hard to keep this distance. He would constantly criticize everyone for almost anything." Dr. Gök's tendency to extend his hand for the younger doctors to kiss after their meetings was an unusual behavior in a professional setting but also understandable given his paternalistic habits, attitudes, and gestures to perpetuate his authority in the Council as well as on campus. During his tenure, he was also accused of working in collaboration with the military regime, covering up the brutal acts of security forces, and creating an expert institution that would make the traces of state violence invisible.

The Süleyman Cihan case in which Dr. Gok participated as a forensic doctor is particularly illustrative of such accusations. Süleyman Cihan, a member of an illegal Communist Party, was taken into custody on July 29, 1981, and tortured to death the next day. An anti-terror police unit denied that he was detained. Meanwhile, the family was frequenting the morgue of the CFM to see photos of unidentified bodies. Finally, with the help of some insider information, the family found the body of Süleyman Cihan in a cemetery for the unidentified. Eighty-two days after his disappearance, the military prosecutor admitted that he had in fact been in detention and said, however, that "he was captured dead."[7] According to the police, he had jumped out of the sixth floor of a building where he was supposedly taken to identify his illegal organization's apartment while under custody (Cihan and Çetin 2011, 141). Süleyman Cihan's brother Ahmet told me that the family was never convinced by this story. To them, he was not the type of person who would commit suicide. He was a dedicated revolutionary.[8]

There were two forensic medical reports for him: a preliminary (pre-autopsy) report dated July 30, 1981, and prepared by doctors who arrived at the crime scene, and the final one, which is based on the autopsy carried out at the CFM (Cihan and Çetin 2011, 135–36, 155–57). The first report indicated that a more detailed autopsy should be performed in order to determine whether the death occurred as a result of a fall or another cause. The detailed autopsy report was prepared at the CFM on August 24, 1981, and was comprised of three parts: external examination, internal examination, and conclusion. The first part of this report identified scars and bruises on the body, which included a burn lesion on the penis. The second part is compiled when the doctor opens the chest, abdomen region, and skull to see if there is any evidence of trauma to the internal organs. After discussing all this evidence, the autopsy report concluded that "the death was brought about by skull fracture, visceral organ damage, and cerebral bleeding that might have happened as a result of a fall from a high place" (Cihan and Çetin 2011, 157). After comparing the final forensic report to that of the preliminary one, the military prosecutor sent an official letter to the CFM asking them to explain why the final autopsy report did not mention the burn lesion on the penis, which was described in the first preliminary forensic report.

Dr. Şemsi Gök did not attend Süleyman Cihan's autopsy. Yet, as the head of the CFM he answered this question in an official letter to the military prosecutor drawing on previous reports and photographs taken during the autopsy. According to this letter, there was no burn lesion on the penis. The first report mistook a scar on the penis that was also mentioned in the first (pre-autopsy) report as a burn lesion. After the death took place, Dr. Gök said, the "scar dried because of the loss of water under the tissue" (Cihan and Çetin 2011, 170). If there were a burn lesion, he claims, the report should have classified the degree of burn, which was not the case. There were a number of indirect consequences of the letter he prepared for the prosecutor. First, the argument he used to explain the burn scar on the penis was not totally unreasonable; it was within the range of possibilities. However, it disregarded the systematic nature of torture in police stations and how electric shock on the genitalia was one of the most common methods of torture inflicted on political prisoners back then. By denying the existence of a burn lesion on the penis and by willingly devising other possibilities, Gök was indirectly *denying* the possibility that the deceased might have been given electroshock to his genitals and he might have been tortured to death under custody. When the prosecutor examined this report and prepared an indictment on the basis of it, he decided not to start a prosecution regarding the police team who detained Süleyman Cihan.

When the lawyers of the family lodged an appeal with the Military Supreme Court in 1985, the military prosecutor again based his arguments on the forensic medicine reports issued by the CFM and signed by Dr. Gök, using the conclusion in the final report: "Death might have occurred as a result of a fall" (Cihan and Çetin 2011, 157). Although the report discussed falling only as a possibility—*might have occurred*—the prosecutor presented the report as establishing solid evidence that Cihan jumped out of the window and committed suicide. Thus, by discussing everything in the range of possibility with the pretense of being more scientific, the report contributed to the regime of denial by making it possible for the prosecutor to defend the denial of torture and death "scientifically." However, this was not the only time that a report would be used for this purpose, nor is this the only interpretation it would give rise to.

From Documenting Scars to Making a Claim for Torture

What makes any official forensic report so important for alternative politics is their potential for reinterpretation. In 2012, when the 1980 coup trials started, the family of Süleyman Cihan wanted to take part in the trials. To this end, they went to Dr. Şebnem Korur Fincancı, who received her specialty in the field of forensic medicine at the Council and worked at the Council for almost a decade, to ask her to prepare a "scientific opinion" on the death of Süleyman Cihan using the photos and previous autopsy reports prepared by CFM. By reinterpreting all the facts written in previous documents, Fincancı's independent report demonstrated that particular findings on the body could be compatible with certain torture methods. After describing these compatibilities, the report stated that the possibility that Cihan might have been thrown out of a window after having been tortured to death cannot be excluded.[9] Given the limited amount of information regarding the conditions of his death and the deficiencies of the autopsy report, this is the most conclusive argument that a forensic expert could make regarding the cause of death.

Süleyman Cihan's case shows how scientific skepticism can be effectively manipulated by doctors in order not to name the violent acts of the state. Equally so, given the fact that the conditions under which crime scene evidence is gathered are controlled by the police and other state actors, alternative reports prepared by doctors fighting for human rights are not irrefutable. In Cihan's case, by introducing other evidence such as eyewitness accounts and testimonies, Cihan's family and friends contextualized his death and took the alternative report as the final evidence of Cihan's death having occurred while he was under police custody. In other words, they introduced sociological and historical data so that the medical report could be interpreted plausibly. How had this happened? How do we account for doctors from the same institution, the CFM, interpreting the same document differently? In this section, I further discuss CFM as a contradictory space that not only produced doctors who contributed to a denial regime with their reports but also trained doctors that would learn to contextualize the reports they were writing for the purpose of torture documentation. Specifically, I narrate how doctors trained by Dr. Gök at CFM have internalized this forensic culture that simultaneously enabled them to both reproduce the denial regime and challenge it at the same time precisely through their investment in the fantasy of medical veracity.

Despite the accusations Dr. Gök faced, he was also seen as a person who holds on to the scientific principles of forensic research and report writing. Even his fiercest critics at the Council would agree that his scientific competence in the field of forensic medicine was unquestionable. Moreover, many of those who challenge the workings of the CFM and question the validity of its reports are also students of Dr. Gök. They were trained, interned, or worked at the CFM. I find the contradiction in Gök's hand extension as a paternalistic gesture and his training legacy that enabled his students to challenge his own competence meaningful and interesting, since this contradiction yields insights regarding the official forensic report-writing practice in Turkey, the specifics of which I examine below to further illuminate how doctors trained by Dr. Gök have internalized this forensic culture that simultaneously enabled them to both reproduce the denial regime and challenge it at the same time precisely through their investment in the fantasy of medical veracity.

Dr. Ahmet was one of these doctors. He was a professor of forensic medicine at a public university before being expelled from his position with an executive order after the coup attempt in 2016 because of his critical and pro–human rights attitude. He volunteered for the Human Rights Association and Human Rights Foundation of Turkey as an independent expert witness on contentious torture, extrajudicial killing, and ill prisoner cases and prepared independent expert reports. He participated in several mass-grave exhumations in the Kurdish region in the first half the 2010s. He is ultimately one of the most important forensic medicine experts on human rights violations in the country, and I have been in touch with him since 2011. When we first met for an interview, I was curious about his experiences at the CFM as an intern, especially about how a progressive pro–human rights doctor could work in the CFM, which leftist and progressive circles consider to be the state's "denial" institution in cases of violence.

Dr. Ahmet decided to specialize in forensic medicine out of his interest in human nature and in social and political matters. He completed his internship at the CFM in 1993 and even worked with Dr. Gök. Many tortured people and people who died under police custody were brought to the Council when Dr. Ahmet was there. So, I asked him what it felt like working at the Council especially when systematic torture cases in police stations and prisons were widespread. Remembering rumors about how some cases of torture were covered up at the Council, he said: "We heard rumors about our professors, about their biased attitude toward political prisoners, but we thought that they were the ultimate professional authorities in forensic medicine and it is an unimaginable thing to question their scientific competence and neutrality. We were seeing them as academic figures and not political ones. However, we slowly realized that this Council was systematically leaving certain things ambiguous when preparing medical reports."

While at the Council, Dr. Ahmet himself performed numerous autopsies on those who died under police custody or were killed during "armed clashes" and "police/military operations." The relatives and the advocates of the dead frequently confronted him and looked at him as if he were an enemy. He further tells: "They look at you as if you are the kind of person who will destroy evidence and misinform people. I thought back then that yes, they can think whatever they like to. This is their most basic right. I don't find it strange. But on the other hand, I thought that they are very ignorant and had no clue about what we were doing." During one of these encounters, some relatives of a deceased person were waiting in front of the morgue door started shouting and cursing at him for "hiding the truth." The accusation to "hide the truth" really made him angry, and he shouted back: "Look, if I wanted to manipulate the findings, you would be completely unaware of that. I would tell you a story with such intricate details that you would not understand that I am lying. So stop staring at me that way and if you want to control what I am doing, bring someone who understands what I am doing."[10] Right after recounting this encounter, however, he told me another story that would confirm the suspicion, fear, and mistrust among relatives of the deceased victims regarding the operations of the Council. He described the gradual changes in how he understood this institution, how he perceived his colleagues who worked as forensic medicine professors, and what he was professionally doing at the CFM: "It was a period in which some people would be 'captured dead'. They would be brought to the Institution. We would detect close shot wounds on the corpse during the autopsy. What does that mean? Let's say the wound is caused by a shot from a distance shorter than 30 centimeters. How can you kill a person from that close if you are not in a bodily fight? It is not possible. It is not reasonable. It has only one explanation. It is an execution. In legal terms, it means voluntary manslaughter."

The real turning point for him was the investigation conducted by the judges from the International Criminal Tribunal for former Yugoslavia that I opened this chapter with. As he tried to explain to these judges the forensic reports-writing practice within which he was trained in Turkey, he also became aware of its limitations and questioned its epistemology. When he and other doctors were performing autopsies, Dr. Ahmet says, they were seeing two-to-five-centimeters-long ecchymosis, some bruises on the back, and many other things. Yet, they would describe these wounds as separate and independent lesions on the body. Despite sensing that what they saw was indeed evidence of torture and could not be something else, they would never write torture as the cause in the report. What he called "a kind of scientific blindness" was behind this unwillingness to conclude torture in the reports: "When we were performing autopsies, we were seeing dead bodies whose hands were tied behind their backs, blindfolded, a single shot in the head entering from behind. The cause of death in this situation can hardly be an accident or a suicide. This is probably a murder. But I would not write that down. I think it was a kind of *scientific blindness* that we had then." In those years, Dr. Ahmet thought that it was the judges that were supposed to enlighten such complicated matters despite the fact that he and others, as doctors, would gather the scientific evidence. Throughout our interview Dr. Ahmet wanted to make sure that I understood how he or his colleagues did not manipulate the findings on the forensic reports when he was working for the Council. The reports by the Council were not wrong in and of themselves. Rather there were structural problems in the system that gave rise to a specific epistemological framework that informed all report-writing practices.

During their training at the CFM, forensic doctors were taught that it was the task of lawyers and prosecutors to investigate and prove the causes behind the wounds and injuries they observed. This also meant that when doctors worked on a case, they did not have access to the details of the context within which the incident took place. Rather, prosecutors and the police monopolized this knowledge. Doctors' responsibility was to answer questions posed by the prosecutor and the judge. These questions forced them to limit their autopsy and examination reports to a certain format where they were somewhat reduced to transmitters of information rather than interpreters of it. This carefully crafted medico-legal report would then shape how medical experts examined their subjects, be it a corpse on the autopsy table or an allegedly tortured person. The doctor examining the body was discouraged from delivering any hint as to what might have caused injuries and harm; in other words, reporting what one saw was the only requirement and, more than this, was somewhat perceived as a form of transgression. Inferring the cause of a particular scar and claiming that the scar was the result of torture would mean destroying the *scientific neutrality* of the profession in general and that of the document in particular.

Beginning in the mid-1990s, many doctors at the CFM gradually realized that the fragmented descriptions of political violence did not have any legal or political consequences unless they were interpreted, commented upon, and used to make an argument in a legal case.[11] One needed a medical expert to analyze and reflect upon these fragmented descriptions of violence so that they could become the evidence of torture. A professor of forensic medicine, Dr. Şebnem Korur Fincancı adamantly believed in such an epistemological shift. "When we started to question our practices in the mid-1990s, almost everyone in the forensic medicine community reacted against us," she said to emphasize the frictions that emerged as they pushed for this epistemological shift. She was one of the first people who objected to this forensic tradition of leaving the commentary section at the end of the reports blank. She was also part of this international forensics team and in fact had written homicide in the commentary section, unlike most forensic doctors from Turkey. According to her, diagnosis of illness requires the analysis of health determinants. This is the only way to propose a proper treatment regimen for any health-related problem. The same holds for the bodily consequences of political violence. If you cannot point to and name the determinants of violence, you cannot eliminate or cure it.

Scientific Suspicion, Official Forensic Epistemology, and the Social Order

Forensic reports lie at the intersection of science, law, and medical expertise. Jasanoff (1995) shows that there are always clashes between the truth-seeking world of science and the justice-serving institutions of law. As Latour (2004) also puts it, scientific and legal practices have different working principles and rely on quite different truth criteria. While the first relies on the idea of suspicion and uncertainty, the latter is based on issuing a swift judgment. The ways these two fields construct their facts and criteria of objectivity are very different from each other. The presumed strict division of labor between law and medicine, the former being the site of evaluation and judgment and the latter being the site of objective and empirical knowledge, has also informed the way politically sensitive forensic reports are prepared in Turkey. In many contexts, the invention of the role of the expert witness has allowed the realm of science and the realm of law to intermingle. Reflecting on the figure of the expert witness, Latour (2004) says that they "occupy the throne of supreme court judges, cloaking their testimony in the incontrovertible authority of the facts as judged" (30). The politicized historical figure of the expert "has the capacity to bring discussion to an end by arrogating to himself the power to bind or unbind by delegating the issue to 'matters of fact.'" According to Latour, scientists can be cast as experts to give opinions and evidence about issues that are within their areas of expertise in front of the court (2010). In his analysis, Latour assumes an inherent distinction between the practice of an expert witness and real scientific work and ignores the larger social and political field within which they both interact. This means that the relationship between science and expert authority is not natural but rather culturally and historically particular. The role of the expert witness required that scientists make certain judgments regarding the conditions under which bodily injuries occurred at least to an extent (Kruse 2016).

Forensic experts in Turkey tend to emphasize the skeptical side of science in their forensic reports and thereby leave the interpretation of the results of their analysis to the prosecutor or judge. They restrict themselves to certain questions raised by the prosecutor and remain within the strictly defined boundaries of science. This type of expert position has had political consequences in the sense that this epistemology becomes constitutive of the state's regime of denial by promoting certain ways of registering facts and discouraging others.

The CFM and forensic reports produced by its doctors embrace an epistemology that draws very much on the aperspectival scientific objectivity that emerged in the mid-nineteenth century and promoted the neutral view. This type of objectivity seeks to eradicate or disregard idiosyncratic and perspectival positions. Forensic medicine experts at the CFM often claim this aperspectival objectivity in their medical-examination practices and autopsy reports by "ignoring all other situational factors entering into the formation of a certain form of knowledge, observation" (Daston and Galison 2007). All that is personal, social, and systematic is avoided in reports prepared by forensic doctors at the CFM. Official forensic epistemology that is embodied by forensic doctors and institutionally and structurally supported by the CFM becomes the source of expert authority. However, the way in which this authority contributes to or challenges the social order is not predetermined. In other words, instead of problematizing the role of expert witness vis-a-vis the scientist, I am interested in how knowledge produced by the expert witness can be empowering or disempowering for marginalized populations depending on the context.

The question of documenting, reporting, and witnessing political violence is an inherently fragile and political task, and it is always open to social conflict and struggle. That is why one needs to conceptualize the expert witness (the forensic doctor in this case) as a historically and politically situated "modest witness" who, as someone working within a series of institutional and political affiliations and hierarchies, is open to manipulation and under the influence of certain prejudices (Shapin and Schaffer 1985). The vital questions become how and with whom expert witnesses will align themselves, which knowledge claims will count as credible and legitimate within medico-legal-techno-scientific institutions, and how the terms of this credibility and legitimacy can be modified, changed, or challenged.

The experiences of progressive forensic doctors in Turkey since the 1980s show us that the boundary between law and medicine is one that is morally and politically drawn and that notions such as "scientificity," "neutrality," and "impartiality" are made and remade through daily encounters. Most forensic doctors who prepare official reports retain a classically skeptical understanding of science in such a way and for so long that torture cannot be called by its name. They leave their analysis at a very abstract and purportedly neutral level by including all kinds of possibilities in their reports. They say they cannot argue for a particular cause if they are not 100 percent certain due to their phantasmal commitment to the politics of veracity. Even though the doctors know that there is more than what they see on a deceased body and on a prisoner's body, it is their fantasies about how forensic reporting should be made that shape their perception of reality of violence.

The "scientific skepticism" and erasure of causality and interference that characterized forensic reports in Turkey has indeed become a very serious problem for victims of violence, their families, and human rights lawyers. One lawyer, Kemal Bilgiç, made a similar observation back in the mid-1990s: "Unfortunately, even if a medical report is positive, the physician does not explicitly state that the signs are due to torture. He just gives objective findings. Since the physicians don't explicitly state that the signs are likely to be the result of torture, the prosecutor argues that the lesions may be due to other reasons. As a lawyer, I would like to see physicians give conclusions of probability, for example, state that there is an 80 percent probability of the cause being such and such" (Physicians for Human Rights, US 1996, 146). The fact that naming torture was systematically avoided under the pretense of being scientific normalized the denial of political violence and contributed to its extension and intensification, especially during the 1990s, when extrajudicial killings and deaths as a result of torture became more systematic and widespread. However, although it is easy to see CFM as a mere instrument of the state used for the purposes of manipulation of facts, the picture is more complicated. For one, despite the dubious nature of CFM reports, some parts of these reports remained a main source of reference for human rights activists who want to prove torture in courts or make it visible via various media. Also, some of the forensic doctors who were trained in this Council later played an important role in the mobilization of forensic knowledge for human rights activism.

This curious situation invites us to examine the workings of forensic denial of torture. This denial mechanism is built on the belief that scientific observation and evidence matter. CFM doctors, even when their political agenda is to support state ideology, follow scientific procedures and methods in their quest for understanding a case of an injured body. This creates a situation where doctors could render violence less invisible without necessarily lying about what they observe and report. These forensic reports carry half-truths about state violence because as medical doctors these experts are invested in forensic fantasies, namely the importance of forensics in finding out the truth for the good of people, and prevent unjust legal decisions and punishments. This epistemological stance is taken up, reproduced, and eventually challenged by the younger generation of forensic medicine specialists. Dr. Ahmet and Dr. Fincancı are just two examples of this. The next chapter examines how doctors who are working in the field human rights took up these partial truths to reveal state violence by focusing specifically the experiences of forensic doctors who began their careers at the CFM and later became the founders of counter-hegemonic, non-governmental organizations in the area of forensic documentation of state violence in Turkey and irreversibly transformed the field of human rights activism and political imagination.

CHAPTER 2

The Proof and Fantasy
of Human Rights

O n August 10, 1993, twenty-nine-year-old university graduate Baki Erdoğan was detained in Aydın, a city in western
Turkey. Charged with being the representative of a radical
leftist organization, he was interrogated incommunicado in Aydın
Police Headquarters for eleven consecutive days. On August 21, he
was taken to a hospital and died there the same day. Shortly after, the
CFM in Istanbul prepared Erdoğan's autopsy report. Despite men-
tioning a long list of cuts and bruises over his entire body, the report
concluded that Erdoğan died of acute pulmonary oedema caused by
a ten-day hunger strike he started under custody to protest police
brutality (Physicians for Human Rights, US 1996, 250).

Upon hearing Baki Erdoğan's death, Dr. Zekiye Ozden, who
was then volunteering for the Human Rights Commission of Izmir
Medical Chamber, formed an investigative team after she secured
permission from the Turkish Medical Association. The team of three
doctors went to Aydın and visited the hospital where Erdoğan died,
talked to nurses and doctors, and interviewed local reporters and
lawyers about the events that took place before his death. To their
surprise, they were given a videotape of Erdoğan's naked body taken
by a wedding cameraman hired by Erdoğan's family before his burial.
In order to analyze all evidence, Dr. Ozden called Dr. Şebnem Korur
Fincancı, who was working as a forensic doctor in the CFM and a

volunteer for human rights organizations at the time, asking if she would work on this case. The latter agreed to help prepare the report in her capacity as a human rights activist. She examined the video, the previous medical reports including the official autopsy report, and the narratives of doctors and nurses. Drawing upon this body of evidence, a group of doctors from Izmir and Istanbul collectively prepared what they called an "alternative report" (*alternatif rapor*), which concluded that Baki Erdoğan was quite likely subjected to torture. As opposed to the official report prepared by doctors in the public hospital and CFM, an alternative report is a report of medical findings by independent doctors at the request of individuals after potential injury that might have taken place under detention. According to Baki Erdoğan's alternative report, his death was caused by adult respiratory distress syndrome, a condition facilitated by certain acts of torture, specifically Palestinian hanging.

Baki Erdoğan's lawyers presented the report to the court as evidence attesting to his death under custody. The report was released with the signatures of volunteer doctors who are affiliated with the Izmir and Istanbul Medical Chambers.[1] Not denying or ignoring the report, the court accepted it as an alternative report and asked for further assessment from the CFM. When this new report came to the CFM's agenda, Dr. Fincancı presented the case by showing Erdoğan's chest radiography and other substantial evidence that linked his death to torture. Dr. Fincancı convinced the other doctors in the commission at the CFM to agree with the findings of the alternative report. As a result, Baki Erdoğan's alternative report became the first official autopsy report that made an explicit commentary on the relationship between police brutality and death under custody as opposed to most forensic reports released by the CFM. The report was drawing upon previous autopsy reports and other medical records yet reinterpreting them in the light of other contextual evidence. The partial truths in forensic reports were mobilized for an alternative reading of Baki Erdoğan's death under custody. Baki Erdoğan's case not only solidified the network of doctors who are working in the field of human rights in different cities of Turkey, but also became the first achievement of medical-expert witnessing against the sovereign rule of the state.

With this case, doctors realized that they could mobilize their medical-expert knowledge on behalf of torture victims in front of a court and lay audience. The court ruled that the deceased undeniably died because of the interrogation under torture.[2] This was unprecedented because for the first time a court accepted a medical report that claimed that torture was the primary cause of death under custody, and the Supreme Court concluded that the autopsy report clearly showed traumatic evidence over the entire body of the deceased. In the last three decades of Turkey, doctors in the field of human rights violations continued to search for forensic medical evidence that could prove these violations. And a fantasy, which I call politicized forensic fantasy, lies behind doctors' commitment to the search of forensic evidence of violence. Trained in the Council and exposed to the forensic fantasies nurtured within it, these doctors, who are working in the field of human rights, have begun to turn these fantasies upside down and use them against the state's security forces. Moved by this fantasy, doctors aimed to put the perpetrators of violence to trial by producing documents about the injured bodies of those targeted by the sovereign power. Doctors fighting for human rights in Turkey have invested in these forensic fantasies in and through their documentation practices against the sovereign state's desire to erase its violence. According to Banu Bargu, "Sovereignty is not the absence of violence, discipline, or domination but the ability to assist their *erasibility* as the ultimate proof of power" (Bargu 2014a, 61). Sovereignty thus works through the politics of erasure that renders "bodies, violence and history invisible; it conceals them behind the façade of law" (Bargu 2014a, 61). The legally sanctioned erasure of violence is formative to sovereign power. As we have seen in the previous chapter, official forensic reports of CFM have been critical to the politics of erasure in Turkey. Doctors who developed an interest in questions of state violence wanted to come to terms with and make visible this politics of erasure hidden behind the façade of law. These doctors were drawn to the gravitational power of jurisdiction through the forensic fantasy that their medical-expert witnessing practices would have critical consequences such as restricting the sovereign power by either bringing perpetrators to trial or "humanizing" their punishment forms.

Most of the doctors involved in torture documentation had experienced an incident of state violence and realized the power of medicine in addressing, resolving, and redressing its consequences. Many of the forensic doctors I followed over the course of my research had developed an interest in torture documentation after witnessing the suffering their friends, comrades, or family members went through in prisons and police stations after the 1980 coup d'état. Not being able to prevent what befell their loved ones, these doctors sought ways of mobilizing their medical knowledge to make their personal witnessing public with the help of their medical expertise. These doctors had gotten to know each other in the branches of human rights organizations and the Turkish Medical Association branches in Istanbul, Ankara, and Izmir and developed ways of proving torture and providing care for torture victims. They were invested in the belief that the "truth" of state violence, that is state crimes, especially that of torture, could be found with the help of forensic documents, and these "truths" would put pressure on bureaucratic, legal, and political structures. Indeed, these stories of initial encounters usually followed up with stories about how their work was instrumental in restricting violence, putting perpetrators to trial, or forcing government authorities to introduce anti-torture procedural guarantees.

Whenever these doctors talked about these initial years, they remembered them as affectively laden moments of collective work and achievements in the field of torture documentation. Doctors told each other and younger generations such stories to keep them committed to the work of torture documentation as these phantasmal narratives would "enable individuals and groups to give themselves histories" (Scott 2012, 51). All this is to underline the fact that forensic fantasies about torture documentation are collective to the extent that they build communities. These forensic-documentation fantasies provide a linear and coherent storyline to doctors about their past practices and connect them to the present. It is through forensic fantasies that the community of medical experts devoted to torture documentation has emerged. The narratives and practices of progressive and pro-human rights doctors that prioritize forensic medicine and forensic documentation in addressing state violence are at the center of this chapter. Forensic fantasies simultaneously informed doctors' counter-hegemonic documentation practices as well as the state's violence practices in terms of its capacity to erase them via official forensic reports. Analyzing historical and ethnographic data about torture documentation in Turkey since the 1980 coup d'état, I discuss the limits and possibilities of radical documentation practices as a political project, showing how doctors' politicized forensic fantasies draw upon the state's power to recognize them as documents of violence. The chapter shows that the proof and fantasy of human rights violations are intertwined, both linked to state violence and the belief in forensic documentation's power to end torture, and further argues that doctors' focus on forensic fantasies overshadows the historical and political dynamics—like encounters with victims and state responses—that sustain these fantasies.

Emerging Intimacies

The pervasive use of torture in police stations and prisons brought the question of torture to the agenda of large sections of society for the first time with the coup.[3] After a few years of silence, the prisoners' families, human rights activists, doctors, and radical political groups started to organize against the widespread and arbitrary use of force in prisons and detention centers. With the narrowing of the popular base of the radical politics or weakening of its claim to alternative sovereignty, human rights emerged as an important and sometimes the only venue to raise a collective voice against state violence.[4] Beginning in the mid-1980s, the governments also began to take concrete legal steps to prevent torture in response to protests and public pressure at home and abroad. These transformations made sense within the broader political dynamics and trends such as Turkey's EU accession process and the then governments' desire to project Turkey as respectful of democracy and human rights. Throughout these moments, civilian and non-civilian governments consistently struggled not to be identified as a "torturer state" (*işkenceci devlet*).[5]

All these developments brought the question of torture, the tortured body, its rights, and torture documentation to the heart of the incipient human rights struggle. In 1986, human rights activists, families of detainees, and political activists founded Turkey's first human rights organization, the Human Rights Association. This association increased the visibility of human rights violations, raised a public voice against torture, and paved the way for the formation of a separate human rights organization dedicated to torture victims. Doctors, who were fighting for human rights, started to use their expertise to document torture and rehabilitate torture victims in the early 1980s in various non-governmental organizations, and these doctors with the help of the Human Rights Association founded the Human Rights Foundation of Turkey in 1990. Since then, the foundation in its relations with torture victims has followed medical humanitarian and human rights principles, providing free medical treatment and documentation work. In sum, beginning with the 1980 coup, we observe the emergence of gradual and spontaneous political and social mobilization of doctors against torture in the name of medical ethics and public health in major cities of Turkey.

The victims of torture resorted to get legal and practical support to file a criminal complaint at the association. The applicants then would be directed to foundation for medical examination, treatment, and documentation purposes. The foundation was strategically located very close to the association. For almost a year, I worked in both of these organizations. I was a volunteer at the Human Rights Association when I decided to connect with the doctors at the foundation in 2012. I made an appointment with the help of a reference, and once there for my meeting, I described my research to members of the foundation. They were very welcoming as my connections at the association must have dissipated the questions that they might have had about me as an outsider doing research on the sensitive topic of torture. Some doctors had academic backgrounds and were therefore eager to listen to my research.[6] I visited the foundation approximately three days a week for a year, and members would also call me when they needed an extra hand or had chores that needed taking care of. I spent most of my days helping them with translation of some medical reports if needed, typing handwritten notes of doctors, and chatting with the secretary and doctors when no applicant was around.

The most striking observation for me at the foundation was the intimate connections between doctors and applicants that were built over the course of years and sometimes decades. One day, as I was helping the medical secretary Gülriz with the organization and classification of the applicant files, two women in their forties holding each other's arms came in. They had just attended the protest in Taksim Square, a major urban space only five minutes from the foundation. They had been badly beaten by the police. Gülriz welcomed them immediately, telling them to sit in the waiting room and asking if they would like to drink water. Then, she called and informed Dr. Leyla about them and reorganized the day's appointments to make sure that they could see a doctor for examination. I realized that the women had been at the foundation before. When they went upstairs to see the doctor, Gülriz told me that these two women had attended the hunger strike in 1996 and were released on medical humanitarian grounds in 2001. Upon release, they had visited the foundation for treatment of their Wernicke-Korsakoff syndrome caused by long term hunger. Yet, their illnesses had not prevented them from participating in political protests. When they got hurt, they already knew where to go to get their scars documented and receive medical care.

After conducting physical examinations and organizing their treatment, Dr. Leyla said goodbye to them. She looked content yet thoughtful as the two women left. Then she turned to me and said, "There is no post-trauma in this country. Trauma over trauma that is all we have." Seeing the foundation's old patients being hurt had made her upset. The ordinariness of this visit struck me a lot because it attested to the affective and intimate relationship that enabled these women to just come in, get their scars documented, and receive treatment. The foundation was like a shelter for those who suffered from or wanted to escape from police brutality. The embeddedness of this foundation among some political activist groups and its centrality for forensic documentation of torture was key to grasping the intimacies produced in clinical encounters.

There is extensive literature on what doctors as medical-expert witnesses can do in the aftermath of violence. Specifically, the centrality of the suffering body in humanitarianism and human rights activism has given the medical profession a privileged role in both attempts to save lives and alleviate suffering in times of crisis or emergency and processes of claims-making and justice-seeking (Abramowitz and Panter-Brick 2015; Ticktin 2014; Robbins 2013; Moyn 2012). These studies point to doctors' differential engagements with the sovereign practices of states, which can be grouped under two main headings. First, doctors can mobilize their expertise for humanitarian purposes in non-governmental organizations by undertaking the task of saving the lives of the sick, the elderly, the wounded, and the tortured (Fassin 2010, 2007; Redfield 2013). This task of saving lives amounts to a sovereign act to the extent that it involves a decision about who has the right to live. However, it does not aim to challenge the sovereignty of the state or replace it with another form of sovereignty. Second, doctors can mobilize their knowledge to produce the truth of violence in the form of medical certificates for refugees to be used in juridical processes (Ticktin 2010; Kelly 2012; Fassin and d'Halluin 2007; Fassin and D'halluin 2008). In most of the cases covered in this scholarship, these certificates aim to expose the violence of sovereign states of the Global South so that refugees can be granted certain legal rights in the countries of the Global North. Even though these doctors produce the proofs of violence, these documents do not have immediate and direct repercussions for the perpetrators who are in another country.

The experiences of doctors in Turkey who work in human rights organizations, public hospitals, and the CFM differ on two important aspects. First, their practices of documentation come with the cost of being criminalized in the eyes of the Turkish state. They face official and non-official forms of threat from security forces or state authorities. Different from doctors who prepare medical certificates in the centers of European capitals, they use their medical expertise against their own state, challenging its sovereignty by producing forensic proofs of human rights violations. As such, their documentation activism has concrete or legal outcomes for the workings of sovereign power such as forcing the police to change the forms of torture they implement or putting the perpetrators of violence on trial.

Most of the doctors I talked to have dedicated their time and energy to torture documentation since the early 1980s or 1990s in various governmental and non-governmental institutions such as the CFM, the branches of the CFM, the Human Rights Foundation of Turkey, the Turkish Medical Association, and medical chambers of Istanbul, Izmir, Ankara, and Diyarbakır. These doctors were in their late twenties or early thirties in the 1980s, often had sympathies for imprisoned or detained political activists or Kurdish people, and were aware of the ongoing state violence in detention centers and prisons. Some of them witnessed the suffering of tortured bodies through their friends or family members and defined themselves as advocates of torture victims and engaged with the field of state violence and torture from an engaged position. What these doctors had in common was that they had developed an attachment to the role medicine can play in the face of torture. Finally, having engaged in the work of documenting different forms of state violence, they observe the repercussions of their work in terms of moderating and restricting police violence. All in all, both these factors put them in an intimate relationship with security forces and the victims of violence. This kind of intimacy raises the stakes of documentation for these doctors. Forensic fantasies draw them toward these intimate relationships because of physical proximity to the incidents, victims, and perpetrators while also acting as a protective shelter for them through the communities and collectives they facilitate.

These intimacies enable us to rethink the relationship between forensic documents, their role as evidence, and their implications for human rights politics because the affordances of these forensic documents are not limited to their role as legal evidence of violence during trials. These documents are sites of emerging intimate relationships between doctors, torture victims, and perpetrators. After all, forensic documents ultimately need interpreters, communities, crowds, networks, political actors, and organizations to create, present, or stage a political truth for or against torture.[7] These doctors' strong practical and emotional investment in this field suggested their strong attachment to this fantasy, which in turn shaped the political field, specifically the field of human rights and state violence. Below, after discussing the emergence of an anti-torture sensibility among doctors in the aftermath of the 1980 coup, I show how this sensibility was gradually translated into a truth-establishment regime in the 1990s with the institutionalization of human rights practice and how doctors found themselves stuck in the dialectics of proof and fantasy of human rights violations where their political subjectivities were tied to their evidence-making capacity and the politics of erasure. Finally, I critically analyze what political forensic fantasies make us forget.

A New Expert Figure Dedicated
to Torture Documentation

Anthropological science and technology studies scholars (Fischer 2003; Fortun 2001; Franklin and Roberts 2006; Knorr-Cetina 1999; Latour 1988; Sunder Rajan 2006) sought to disperse the aura of the expert and expertise and show how expert knowledge is situated within the wider network of social and historical relationships. There is now a wealth of research that underlines the social and cultural processes that gave rise to the formation of professional expert identity, focusing on the interactional, performative, and situated nature of expertise (Carr 2010; Matoesian 2008). Most of these studies, however, tend to be rationalist in their core (Boyer 2008). Only few studies have examined sentiments, affects, and aspirations to humanize experts or moved beyond the confines of their professional habitus (Gusterson 1996). Building on these, I broaden our understanding of expert identity beyond the prevalent constructivist and rationalist tendencies of existing theories by transposing socio-scientific uses of fantasy and arguing that expert identity is constituted in relation to the broader collective and political will of which they feel a part. It is through the lens of forensic fantasy that we better understand the subjectivities of doctors who witness and take a stand against violence against all odds.

Even though these doctors are all medical experts and their engagement with human rights activism has been primarily through their expertise, this cognitive aspect fails to account for their commitment to torture documentation and the strength of their identities as human rights activists (Glynos 2001; Goodwin 1994). The feelings of excitement and solidarity that dominated these doctors' interactions and meetings seemed crucial to understand the nature of their human rights activism vis-à-vis state violence in Turkey. We have witnessed the emergence of a vibrant literature that examines the formation of expert cultures, practices, and subjects in a wide range of fields in Turkey including industrial production, agriculture, energy, security, medicine, law, bureaucracy, and civil society (Babül 2017; Akarsu 2018; Dole 2020; Kayaalp 2015; Silverstein 2020). By centering affects, fantasies, and ideologies to the heart of our analysis of clinical encounters between doctors and victims of state violence, I want to complicate our understanding of the role of medical experts and the truth of violence in redressing injury and harm (Kelly 2015).

These feelings became most palpable to me when I entered one of the lecture halls at Istanbul University's medical school for Dr. Şebnem Korur Fincancı's last lecture titled "Human Rights and Doctor Responsibility" during her retirement ceremony.[8] As a renown forensic doctor in the field of torture documentation with an extensive network and experience, Dr. Fıncancı was greeting everyone with a big and proud smile on her face. Far from holding a depressed atmosphere, the lecture hall was buzzing with laughter and incessant talk as old friends, comrades, and colleagues were seeing and hugging each other. The strong ties of comradeship, collegiality, and camaraderie among these doctors were palpable in the air. Dr. Fıncancı's students who worked as forensic medicine doctors in the clinics of emergency wards for mandatory detainee examination, her friends from medical school who worked as professors at forensic medicine departments, and her doctor and activist friends from human rights organizations and professional medical associations were all there. Even her friends from the Council were there. What these doctors had in common was not only the importance they attributed to the truth revealed with the help of forensic documents, but also the emotional attachment to and affection they had for each other and to the human rights movement.

Her moving and rhetorically powerful speech started with a story from her training days at the CFM in the 1980s. I had listened to this story several times during our previous meetings. It was about the body of a radical leftist activist who died under custody and was brought to the Council for autopsy. Professors at the Council who did this autopsy sought to account for scars on the body with causes other than torture. Shocked with how professors sought to render violence on the body invisible, she promised herself to speak the truth. Defining herself as a follower of social medicine tradition, she argued that political violence was a public health problem and should be approached as an epidemic. For her, social medicine united medical and political thought, and, quoting Rudolph Virchow, she said: "Medicine is a social science, and politics is nothing more than medicine on a grand scale." Therefore, doctors should be "attorneys for the poor," for those who were subjected to violence, and for those who were suffering. This, to her, should be central to medical ethics.

The acts of torture occupied a special place in imagining and practicing human rights struggles in Turkey. Especially in the aftermath of the 1980 coup d'état, political mobilization around the use of torture against dissident groups produced a left-wing and progressive human rights movement. As the scale and scope of torture practices expanded, those who wanted to show solidarity with the tortured, such as the families, progressive intellectuals, politicians, and human rights activists, organized meetings and campaigns, released press statements, prepared petitions, visited state officials in protest of torture, and followed court cases where defendants made torture allegations. Rather than making a claim to an alternative sovereignty as in the case of radical socialist or nationalist political organizations (Bargu 2014b), the incipient human rights movement was foregrounding the rights of individuals, especially the right to life. This was resonating well with the slogan that became popular during prison resistances against torture among leftist prisoners in the aftermath of 1980 coup d'état: "Human dignity shall overcome torture" (İnsanlık onuru işkenceyi yenecek).

The notion of "human dignity" played a crucial role in the development and expansion of human rights discourses and anti-torture struggles beginning in the 1970s. Even though the notion of dignity is not a fully stable notion with a fixed meaning (Bornstein and Redfield 2011, 18–20), it has remained in circulation within leftist circles as well as among human rights defenders up until today. It is still extensively used in meetings, press statements, and political brochures concerning torture, and the members of certain leftist political groups are known to shout this slogan when they are subjected to police brutality. Even those who show solidarity with the tortured at the courts, in front of prison gates, and in meetings also use this slogan. While the slogan attributes a progressive ethical value to the fight against torture, dignity as an abstract notion is presented as the source of empowerment for the person under torture. Overall, the slogan is an emblem of the inclusive nature of anti-torture mobilization in the country.

As the protests against torture increased along with the public pressure at home and abroad between the years 1986–1988 (Göregenli and Özer 2010; Amnesty International 1989), the then government began to take some legal steps against torture, which were deemed critical to the official project of building a civilian rule in the country with its properly working parliamentary system and democratic institutions after the coup. Amnesty International published its first report on torture in Turkey in 1985. This report was based on testimonial evidence gathered from political refugees in Europe or interviews with experts in Turkey regarding the severity of the torture situation. Shortly after, the government approved the European Human Rights Convention in 1987 and gave citizens the right to make individual applications to the European Human Rights Commission. Within this period, Turkey signed two other important international conventions against torture. The first one was the United Nations' Convention Against Torture and Inhuman and Degrading Treatment or Punishment, which Turkey signed in 1988 and which was enacted the same year. The second one is the European Convention Against Torture, which was also signed, approved, and entered into force same year. The government also made some substantial revisions in the criminal code in line with its project to create an image of the country as being democratic and respectful of human rights principles and regulations. One of the election promises of the mainstream Motherland Party (Anavatan Partisi, ANAP) at the time was the founding of the Ministry of Human Rights in 1992. The ministry was not founded after the elections, yet one of the state ministers was declared to be human rights minister. Facing international and domestic pressure because of mounting torture records, that same year the government also prepared and passed a new law of criminal procedure to show that it is respectful of human rights. However, in practice this did not lead to any significant changes because those who were tried in State Security Courts (Devlet Güvenlik Mahkemeleri)—who are most likely to have been tortured—were kept exempt from most of the progressive procedures of this regulation. Finally, in 1994, the then prime minister Mesut Yılmaz published a circular order titled "End to Torture." All in all, the government's declaration of allegiance to human rights principles via the ratification of international treaties as well as other national regulations against torture empowered human rights activists.

These were also the years in which human rights activism could find global support as human rights treaties were—at least discursively—backed by the United States (Moyn 2010). It is within this context that doctors developed a vested interest in questions of torture and the physical and mental well-being of tortured people. Especially doctors with a background in public health or progressive health movements played an important role in creating this sensibility about the challenges that awaited torture victims upon their release from prison or detention. These doctors wanted to figure out their rights and responsibilities in the face of state violence by resorting to international guidelines and conventions regarding medical ethics.

Let me start with the story of Dr. Nusret Fişek. Dr. Fişek single-handedly created a strong rationale and ground for doctors who wanted to work in the field of human rights well before the founding of the Human Rights Foundation of Turkey in 1989 with the sole purpose of treating torture victims and documenting torture. As a retired public health professor and a senior bureaucrat, he became the head of the Turkish Medical Association, doctors' semi-autonomous and semi-formal national professional organization, between 1983 and 1990.[9] Dr. Fişek mobilized the organizational capacity of the Turkish Medical Association in favor of those subjected to various human rights violations. Due to its half-private and half-public status, the Turkish Medical Association had a relative autonomy as a public institution. Moreover, it had a privileged and respected position in society, and its members could easily get an appointment with state officials to discuss human rights issues such as human rights violations in prisons, torture allegations, and so on.

Dr. Fişek objected to capital punishment and protested doctors' presence during the implementation of this punishment by writing a letter to the members of the parliament on behalf of this association. When he was put on trial for this letter, he defended himself by quoting international medical institutions' resolutions (specifically the World Health Organization's 1981 resolution), international documents such as Lisbon or Tokyo Protocols[10] and medical professionals ethics code. In his defense, the Turkish Medical Association also released statements objecting to adverse living conditions in prisons, forced feeding of hunger strikers (or not providing them with sugared water), or the presence of law enforcement officers in doctors' room during the health examination of detainees.[11] Dr. Fişek believed that a doctor should approach the health problems of detainees or prisoners from a perspective of public health; accordingly, he considered torture to be first and foremost a public health issue impacting large sections of society, impairing them physically and mentally. For him, torture and bad treatment were unacceptable, and the Turkish Medical Association could play a role in the struggle against them. Dr. Fişek was one of the first doctors who systematically reflected on what doctors' attitude should be in the face of state violence.[12] His progressive interpretation of principles of medical ethics from a human rights perspective pushed the branches of Turkish Medical Association in different cities toward a more progressive line, especially the Ankara, Istanbul and Izmir Chambers of Medicine. As a result, sporadic efforts of doctors against torture gradually institutionalized beginning in the mid-1980s with the help of these chambers.

The Human Rights Commission of the Izmir Medical Chamber occupied a special place in the anti-torture mobilization in Turkey. This commission was founded by a group of doctors who are interested in human rights problems in the country from a medical perspective. Izmir, located in the western part of Anatolia, is especially known for its close-knit network of doctors working in the field of human rights. Since the mid-1980s, these doctors organized under the medical chamber and were increasingly drawn to the scenarios where they find out, document, and show the violence hidden or denied by state officials. One of the most important figures in this early institutionalization efforts was Dr. Veli Lök, who was a world-renowned orthopedic trauma specialist affiliated with the Izmir Medical Chamber. His name came up whenever I talked to doctors about the field of torture documentation. For my interview, I visited him in his private clinic in Izmir, which he had opened after he retired from his position at the Department of Orthopedics and Traumatology in Ege University. Our interview started after he finished kindly talking to the last patient in his office. I learned that Dr. Lök's engagement with human rights struggles began shortly after his son was tortured in prison in the late 1970s. Feeling desperate that he could not prevent what befell his son, he began thinking of ways to use medical procedures and techniques to detect physical signs of torture long after the abuse had occurred. To that end, Dr. Lök and some of his friends took a novel and radical step, bringing together a group of medical specialists under the Examination and Reporting Sub-commission (Muayene ve Rapor Altkomisyonu) under the Human Rights Commission (İnsan Hakları Komisyonu) of the Izmir Medical Chamber in 1989. This was the first group formed in Turkey with the sole purpose of preparing medical reports after examining the applicant and making torture visible as opposed to sovereign power that aims to erase it. This commission was forming up a team of experts specializing in relevant disciplines to prepare the report and sign it with the chamber's letterhead. Their purpose was to ensure that the scientificity and objectivity of these forensic reports would not be questioned and their chances of being accepted as evidence at courts would increase. When I asked him about how they came up with this idea of using medicine for torture documentation, he said: "As doctors, we must object to all kinds of acts that hurt people's health. We start our profession with this oath. But our hands are most of the time tied in the face of torture. We cannot perform our profession. Doctors try to diagnose torture such as falanga or beatings with their naked eye, mere observation, which is the simplest instrument of medicine. Knowing this, perpetrators of torture try to extend [the] detention period so that ecchymosis on the body disappear and become invisible."

The rest of his narrative was about how they tried different medical diagnosis techniques to scientifically prove torture as the police kept changing its torture methods. Dr. Lök and his friends first began to think if it would be possible to diagnose tissue-level changes under ecchymosis—caused by torture—with a needle biopsy. This procedure turned out to be ineffective. Later, he and his colleagues decided to use a bone-scintigraphy method to detect signs of torture on bones. With this method, they were able to determine if someone was subjected to falanga torture even when there were no external signs on the soles of the feet. For Dr. Lök, this invention immediately impacted how enforcement officials inflicted violence on detainees, at least in the Izmir area. He explained: "As we prepared reports based on scintigraphy proving if falanga was used on soles, more and more police officers working in our region began to face trials. Then they were overcome with panic and in a year or two the police stopped using falanga torture at all." However, this did not mean that torture came to an end in that region. Dr. Lök continued: "After a short while we realized that the number of people suffering from testis twisting torture who applied to our commission in Izmir increased rapidly. Then, we used a dynamic scintigraphy method to diagnose and prove testis-twisting torture. In response, the police switched their methods again and began using electrical torture widely. In order to prove electrical torture, we decided to apply needle biopsies on the burn lesions where the electric shock was implemented. After this, the police began to appear before the court due to electric torture allegations."

His was a story of a back-and-forth relationship between doctors as medical experts and the police as force experts around the question of demonstration and erasability of violence. This story was conveying the message that as doctors developed new techniques to detect torture, the modalities of state violence also transformed and the police response got more sophisticated. Moreover, he also made the argument that once the use of torture was proven, there was the possibility of legal consequences such as putting the perpetrators to trial. Over the course of my research, doctors repeatedly told this story or similar stories where doctors' medical witnessing has had legal or practical repercussions in terms of restricting or transforming state violence.

This was the motivation for many doctors in those years. For example, Dr. Ayşe, who works as a forensic doctor in the CFM, has also been working in the field of human rights. When I asked her how she decided to specialize in forensic medicine, she told me about her family. Raised in a Kurdish and leftist family, she grew up listening to the stories of state violence and developed an interest in human rights. She was a young doctor in the aftermath of the 1980 coup d'état and couldn't help but got involved in the incipient human rights struggle. She participated in a circle of doctors who organized to provide medical care for torture victims in private clinics or public hospitals that they were working in. What mattered for her then "was to be useful, to be able to do something useful for those who went through torture." She decided to become a forensic medicine expert, thinking that "fascism can change anything except medicine."

Despite coming from a right-wing and pro-state family, Dr. Ozden also decided to dedicate her life to human rights activism when she was a fourth-year medical student. I had interviewed her in the Izmir branch of the foundation. When I asked her how she decided to specialize in forensic medicine, she told me about how she was struck with the torture stories of her leftist friends' and how some doctors treated them badly under custody or in prison. She was not a member of any political organization, yet she felt angry and depressed about doctors' complicity in violence. Then one day she heard from a friend about torture rehabilitation centers in the United States where doctors, psychologists, or psychiatrists provide medical treatment and support for torture victims. This, to her, was "mind-blowing." She felt that she knew what to do for the rest of her life. She started to read about revolutionary doctors in Latin America and debates around doctors' responsibility in the face of torture. After graduation, she started to work in a small hospital in a provincial city for her compulsory medical service. Yet, she couldn't complete her service there because she was asked to ignore the scars of a beating and ecchymosis on the body of a detainee brought by the police. Facing political pressure, she quit her official position and mandatory service and began to search for ways of getting involved in human rights activism as a medical doctor. Hearing about the newly opened Human Rights Foundation of Turkey, which aimed to provide rehabilitation and documentation for torture victims, she went to Ankara to work there in 1990. They could not hire her, but they suggested that she work in the Izmir branch when it opened. When it opened the following year, she started to work as a medical secretary and coordinator doctor both for the Examination and Reporting Commission at the Izmir Medical Chamber and the Human Rights Foundation of Turkey. In a sense, she became the focal point connecting different medical non-governmental organizations in Izmir.

Long before I met Dr. Ozden, I had already heard how she was a key person in doctors' anti-torture struggles in the Izmir area. So, I asked her thoughts about doctors' role in human rights struggles. For her, the question that lay at the heart of the human rights struggle was how "to make the apparent evincible/demonstrable (*Her şey açıkken nasıl gösterilebilir olur*)," and this was possible with doctors because "saying that torture exists doesn't mean anything unless you make it visible scientifically." I wanted her to elaborate: "When a person says that he was tortured, no one believes him. But when a doctor says a person was tortured and these are the medical findings of torture, it is different. Scientific experiments or scientific reports are verifiable and repeatable. So independent of who does the research, the result is the same. All doctors will get the same result. The x-ray and scintigraphy of male genitalia will show testis twisting torture and whoever reads these reports will come up with the same diagnosis."

That is how, she said, they concluded that their struggle should target the state's denial regime that systematically concealed its violence. The challenging task of these doctors is to oppose the historically constructed regime of denial and its intricate politics of erasure by documenting torture. Dr. Fincancı once told me a story that summarizes this official politics of erasure. A woman visited the foundation for examination ten days after she was released from detention and said that she was subjected to electric shocks. But doctors could not find any mark on her body because the police had splashed water all over her body during torture sessions to prevent torture marks. But after learning that she had underwear on during the electric torture, Dr. Fincancı asked her to show her back and realized that there was a tiny spot just under the metallic clasp of her bra because it had remained dry during electric torture. She decided to perform a biopsy on that spot. The biopsy proved there had been electric current. In another case, she was examining a man who said he was also given electric shock with a wire from the foot. After searching for a spot on the foot in vain, Dr. Fincancı saw a tiny dot between his fourth and little toe. She carried out a biopsy on that dot, and that proved the electric torture had occurred.

Doctors working in the human rights field told similar stories during interviews, in conferences and training workshops, or in written reports of torture documentation and the techniques and methods that they developed to detect torture. These stories of documentation were often narrated in a detective-story genre in which doctors emerged as figures who managed to prove torture despite the police's tactics to deny it. The police officers, prosecutors, and politicians could all deny the existence of torture, but there was nothing they could do when faced with the scientific evidence of torture. In these stories, doctors found a way to undeniably prove torture. Their formal and informal networks and the stories that they told to themselves and each other had prepared doctors to know how to produce the knowledge of the tortured body against the state's denial regime and convinced them of the importance of their work, which kept forensic fantasies alive.

All in all, the early 1980s were special in the history of political mobilization in Turkey as doctors coming from different specialties sought ways to contribute to addressing human rights struggles. Acting as what Foucault (1984) called "specific intellectuals," they mobilized their specialist medical knowledge to document torture. This was a period in which a new doctor figure who is dedicated to make the invisible torture visible by deploying medical instruments, techniques and discourses emerged. By the end of 1980s, the semi-formal and semi-structured anti-torture networks among doctors, human rights activists, and political activists had slowly but surely formed through word of mouth and personal relations in Istanbul, Ankara, and Izmir.[13] However, the idea of approaching the body of the political activist as the object of medical gaze in the name of human rights was a novel practice that created resistance among political activists. The next section deals with the challenges of implementing the medical gaze in encounters with "torture victims" who do not consider themselves "victim" at all in these institutionalized settings.

How Encounters and Networks Nurture a Fantasy

While searching for institutional ways of documenting torture, the doctor members of the Human Rights Association began to discuss the need to have an independent medical-expert institution dedicated to the rehabilitation of torture victims and documentation of torture. They launched the Human Rights Foundation of Turkey which since then has been working in collaboration with the Human Rights Association as well as Turkish Medical Association to provide treatment for the victims of torture, trace the evidence of torture in the stories and bodies of victims, and write this information down in the form of a medical report.

At first, doctors at the foundation or association did not know how to conduct interviews with the victims of torture or how to carry out medical investigations of torture. It was through clinical exchanges with ex-prisoners and political activists that they became informed about the subjectivities and sensitivities of the people who were subjected to state violence. Most interestingly, political activists who were tortured in police stations or during protests tended to downplay the physical and psychological scars of torture. This was understandable given that many radical leftist groups constructed their post-coup identity through their resistance to torture. Similarly, they identified their political mobilization with political figures who "did not break under torture" in the 1960s and 1970s.[14]

Understood mostly as the state's counterinsurgency tactic to elicit confession from the members of radical organization, one's resistance under torture was regarded as authentic evidence of that person's devotion to his or her political ideology. Many political activists thus did not find it necessary to see a doctor to get their scars documented except for purposes of treatment. This idea of resisting torture with dignity remained a popular idea among leftist groups even after the coup. In accordance with this perception, torture was not considered a shocking, exceptional, or traumatizing experience for them. On the contrary, as political activists, they had already taken the risk of torture once they mobilized against the state.

The biggest challenge for doctors in the beginning was thus to convince political prisoners that their bodily or psychological pain caused by torture mattered and that they might need professional help regarding the physical as well as psychological trauma of torture. Political activists were in a sense refusing to be reduced to an object of medical gaze. Certain political organizations for example required their members to get permission from the organization before accepting therapeutic support from the foundation. And when they ended up visiting the foundation to get their torture experience documented or receive medical care for their bodily injuries, the biggest site of contention between doctors and applicants concerned the question of whether the applicant should see a psychiatrist or a psychologist regarding their torture experience.

According to the doctors at the foundation, many radical political groups and activists gradually understood the importance of medical documentation of torture and changed their position on torture documentation and rehabilitation support. Once political activists were convinced that medical documentation of their scars was important, they also started to invest in forensic fantasies (See Chapter 4). One such political prisoner was Mehmet. He was released from prison after twelve years. He had heard about the Human Rights Foundation of Turkey yet couldn't exactly figure out its purpose. Thanks to his extensive reading in prison, he said, he had moved beyond dominant perceptions about torture that strictly

focused on whether one "confessed," "broke," or "resisted" under torture. Yet, he still couldn't understand why political prisoners needed
to see doctors as if they were "patients" needing treatment. What
was the point of documentation if everyone already knew that the
state tortured political activists in police stations or prisons? During
our interview in the office of the foundation, I asked him what he
and other political prisoners thought about the foundation when
they first heard about it. He said: "We were curious about what, if
anything, medical treatment had to do with torture." Ten days after
his release in 1991, Mehmet along with some of his friends paid a
visit to the foundation to see what their work was about.

At the time, Dr. Ozden was working both as a medical secretary
and a doctor there, and she told them about the foundation and its
purpose. After listening to her, Mehmet agreed to see the doctor and
the psychiatrist at the foundation. Even though his treatment did
not last long, these encounters completely changed his perspective
on medical treatment of torture victims and documentation of torture. He was impressed with the doctors' work and began to visit
the foundation regularly to help them with chores. He soon started
to work there as a medical secretary. Mehmet's story shows how
doctors' fantasies about documentation proved to be effective in
convincing political activists to participate in documentation as a
meaningful way to struggle against torture, while also boosting doctors' forensic fantasies.

For Dr. Ozden political prisoners cultivated "very sophisticated,
collective and solidaristic ways of dealing with the destructive consequences of torture," and it was through the encounters with them
that they also elaborated their methods and manners as doctors,
specifically, what to pay attention to during physical and psychological examinations. Over the years, by learning to recognize their sensitivities and letting them become active agents during the interview,
doctors established a rapport with many applicants who were also
political actors with diverse political backgrounds. When discussing
how they synthesized their medical knowledge with the applicants'
sensitivities, Dr. Ozden firmly situated their practice against those

who committed torture: "In a rehabilitation center, you must do the exact opposite of what the torturer or the state official tries to do in a detention center. If they try to scare and intimidate people, your task is to make them feel supported. If their message is to keep them away from people, our task should be to try to get closer to them and remain in solidarity with them." Similar to how medical reports are seen as an antidote to the state's denial regime, Dr. Ozden envisions doctors' attitudes as the exact opposite of those of torturers. They should be on political prisoners' sides, working for them and with them. Dr. Yasemin, who was working in Istanbul branch of the foundation, also said that the applicants should know that they could stop the process anytime during her interviews with them. She was inspired by the human rights paradigm of public health and forensic medicine departments when she was a medical school student after having attended a seminar on "human rights and the role of doctors" organized by Dr. Ata Soyer.[15] When I asked her about patient examinations, she said that her priority was to convey the feeling that they are in charge and that's why a doctor asks for the patient's consent at every stage of the interview.

Doctors in different branches of the foundation told me about their attitude toward the applicants with almost the same sentences. When interacting with the applicants,[16] their priority is to convey feelings of trust and transparency to them. Political activists who applied to the foundation began to invest in forensic fantasies only after being assured that the medical gaze of doctors did not strip them of their political identities. Similarly, certain political groups, factions, and activists sustained long-term solidarity with the doctors at the foundation. These activists viewed the foundation as a place where their bodily injuries could be treated while contributing to its forensic archive. Regardless of the extent and manner in which these political groups were invested in forensic fantasies, these long-term relationships kept the forensic fantasy alive by making their suffering bodies and experiences available to doctors.

In the early 1990s, the documentation-centered political activism of doctors was gaining traction in Istanbul as well. For example, the Human Rights Association and the medical chamber in Istanbul initiated a campaign to increase the number of applicants who would share their experiences of torture. The campaign invited victims of torture to their offices to be the witnesses and evidence of torture. The project was announced with a press release entitled "Alternative Reports for Torture" on March 13, 1992. This was framed as a strategy against the state's denial of torture through the CFM. The press release read as follows:

> Medical documentation of torture has always been a controversial issue in Turkey. Council of Forensic Medicine and its branches have the authority to prepare official reports for all legal cases, including the ones concerning torture. It is just normal that one expects an Institution endowed with such important powers to have a modus operandi that is independent of political authorities and rumors. But, to put it mildly, it is "extremely controversial" to say that Council of Forensic Medicine in Turkey has these qualities. . . . Documentation of torture is such an important subject that it cannot be left to such "controversial" institutions. That is why, as two non-governmental organizations that have taken initiatives in the struggle against torture, we have decided to collaborate on the documentation of torture. To this end, the Istanbul Medical Chamber has formed a commission of specialist doctors. The reports prepared by this Commission will test official reports at courts, and in public. Such alternative reports will be an important step in the exposure and prevention of denial of torture.[17]

In the remainder of the statement, all tortured people were urged to apply to these human rights organizations where they were examined by a team of independent medical experts not affiliated with the CFM. Here, we again see the power attributed to the documentation as a strategy to fight the state's systematic denial of torture. Doctors working in human rights and medical professional organizations invited tortured people to come under the sight of their medical gaze. In its conclusion, the statement highlights: "The struggle against torture should ignore distinctions between the political and apolitical, leftist and rightist. The most important thing in this struggle is the documentation of torture." Despite the divisions among political fractions working in the Human Rights Association back then, the release of this statement showed the consensus among different political groups around the importance of medical evidence to fight torture. These are strong echoes of forensic fantasies among both political activists and human rights activists.

Doctors at different branches of the Human Rights Foundation of Turkey established long-term relationships with their applicants, and this enabled them to develop novel strategies of forensic documentation of violence. These applicants were mostly either members of leftist political parties and/or of Kurdish origin, and each time these politically "dangerous" people faced torture under police custody and in prison, they would visit human rights organizations. The number of applicants at the medical chambers and the foundation increased especially after the release of the majority of political prisoners in 1991. Doctors at the foundation referred to ex–political prisoners as chronic applicants as many of them were suffering from torture-related chronic or long-term illnesses. One of the tasks of doctors was to figure out if these chronic illnesses were caused by ill or bad treatment they were subjected to under detention or in prison. The clinical examination of such cases was usually longer as these prisoners tended to have a longer history of encounters with state violence and were more likely to have suffered from different types of violence over an extended period. Besides chronic applicants, the foundation also received acute applicants, who needed immediate medical care as their scars and pain were recently created due to torture in a police station or on the streets. The examination of these people at the branches of Human Rights Foundation of Turkey and the medical chamber are usually done as soon as possible to ensure that all signs of torture could be registered before they disappeared.

To increase their chances of demonstrating a reasonable connection between bodily scars and violent acts of security forces during
the protests, in prisons, under custody, or in house raids, doctors
in Izmir came up with the idea of "healthiness reports" (*Sağlıklılık
raporu*) in the mid-1990s. They were preparing reports for people
when they were healthy before their encounters with the police or
before they were sent to prison. Dr. Emin, an internal medicine specialist in the Human Rights Commission of Izmir Medical Chamber,
explained how this report format emerged. At the time, there were
lots of stories regarding how security forces or undercover police
would threaten, follow, or take into custody dissident members from
especially Kurdish or radical leftist groups. Doctors were going to
prepare healthiness reports for those who felt that they were being
followed by undercover policeman. Similarly, these reports were
intended for those who would attend a risky protest where the police
would likely use force on protestors or take them into custody. They
started to wonder if they could prepare counter-documents about
the body before torture took place. So, they came up with this idea of
healthiness reports, which would demonstrate that a certain person
was a healthy individual on a given date before his/her encounter
with the police. If torture took place during their encounters with
the police, these same people could come back for another round of
medical examination. Having two medical reports of an individual
prepared before and after custody allowed doctors to argue that it
was very likely that these scars took place under custody, namely
after that person received the "healthiness report." The healthiness
report was bringing the body of the political activist to the center
of a struggle against state violence by objectifying it in the form of
a medical report. The healthiness report has been one of the novel
modes of alternative report-writing practice inspired by and in turn
contributed to the forensic fantasy.[18]

Doctors in the field of human rights violations used medical witnessing to analyze and objectify the body strategically in the broader
fight against the regime of systematic state violence and its denial.
They convinced political activists to become the witnesses of torture
or to receive healthiness reports in human rights organization as a

political practice. It is their encounters with political prisoners and doctors who are committed to see, analyze, and report their torture-related suffering that kept forensic fantasies alive. These fantasies were consolidated in the form of a working manual in 1999, which I examine below.

Consolidation of Forensic Fantasies

The story of Baki Erdoğan that opened this chapter connected doctors working in the field of human rights in Izmir, Istanbul, and Ankara, and paved the way for the preparation of the first alternative medical report. As a result of this incident, doctors realized that their forensic-documentation practices might have legal and political outcomes for the perpetrators of violence. Another dramatic torture incident, which took place in Manisa in 1995, strengthened these doctors' belief in the political and legal efficacy of forensic medical witnessing. This incident quickly came to the public attention thanks to the work of journalists, reporters, and members of the parliament and enabled the formation of formal and informal networks among doctors located in different cities. This incident also generated the first steps of a practical manual for torture documentation later known as the United Nation's Istanbul Protocol: Manual on the Effective Investigation and Documentation of Torture and Other Cruel, Inhuman or Degrading Treatment or Punishment.

In 1995, sixteen young people—some of them under eighteen years old—were taken into custody as part of an operation against a radical leftist organization in Manisa, a city located in the Aegean region of Turkey. Some of them were accused of painting anti-fascist slogans on a school wall. They were detained and brought to Manisa Police Headquarters. Shortly after, families began to hear rumors that their sons and daughters were being tortured under detention. Under custody, the detainees had seen doctors several times, but none had been properly examined. After spending approximately two weeks under custody, all of them were sent to prison while they waited for their trial. Lawyers made official requests to send these

young people to a full-fledged hospital for health examinations and
documentation purposes, but these requests were denied. Afraid
that the scars of torture would disappear before they were released
from the prison, the doctors at the Izmir branch of the Human
Rights Foundation of Turkey and the Izmir Medical Chamber came
up with an idea. They would ask defendants to write down their torture stories and show the size and type of the scar they had on their
body by using a piece of paper that had a body figure. According to
Dr. Ozden, they wanted to fight against time by collecting detailed
stories of torture accompanied by the diagrams to carefully examine the compatibility between their stories and bodily scars before
the latter would disappear. The purpose was to be able to prove at
the court that the police tortured the young people under custody,
and then try the perpetrators. The lawyers had a plan to document
torture that required the collective effort of all organizations and the
contributions of the imprisoned youth. As Leyla, one of the lawyers
of these young people, explained to the detainees in prison:

> We ask you to fill out anatomical atlases provided by the
> Human Rights Foundation of Turkey. After collecting them,
> we will seek expert opinions from doctors. For now, all we
> ask is for you to write down all of your complaints by mark-
> ing this atlas. Include all complaints such as bruises, purple
> spots, ecchymosis, etc. Write in detail about whatever was
> done to you while in custody. Don't miss a thing. Specialist
> doctors will examine your writings and diagrams. At the
> same time, we want to ensure that you are taken to a fully-
> equipped hospital before the marks of torture on your body
> disappear. The opposing side will try to delay this process.
> Once you are at the hospital, everything will come to light.
> It is important that you follow these instructions until you
> reach the hospital. It is crucial for us to be able to file a case
> against the police who tortured you.

Following Leyla's call, these young people wrote very long narratives
and filled out these anatomical atlases very carefully. After collecting

the drawings and detailed stories of torture, the Examination and Reporting Commission of the Izmir Medical Chamber prepared thorough medical reports with a commentary. Dr. Ozden remembers the report-writing process as an extremely anxiety-driven one. Doctors felt that they were navigating an unknown field because even though they knew these young people were tortured, they were not sure how to prove it scientifically. Using an anatomical atlas as a practical device to mark tortured body parts formed the first step in producing a universal and mobile manual to detect and document torture.

Doctors' knowledge on human rights violations and their documentation got more sophisticated and professionalized after 1994. Professional activities that aimed to disseminate forensic-documentation knowledge—specifically about how to use forensic medicine and forensic reporting in primary care settings such as emergency wards—among practitioner doctors proliferated. The Turkish Medical Association organized various symposia such as "Human Rights and Doctors' Responsibility" in 1995 and "Medicine and Human Rights" in 1996, during which standards for forensic examination in the form of an international guidebook began to take shape. The Istanbul Protocol is designed as a counterpart to the Minnesota Protocol, a manual for a medico-legal investigation of extralegal, arbitrary, and summary executions. The Istanbul Protocol establishes international guidelines for the effective investigation and documentation of torture, setting out scientific and technical diagnostic tools to investigate and document human right violations as they appear on living bodies. The United Nations endorsed the protocol in 1999. As an important pillar of domestic and international torture-monitoring mechanisms, the protocol establishes a guide regarding how physical and psychological consequences of torture should be recorded in a medico-legal report, how the physical scars should be photographed and analyzed, under what conditions consultations from other medical specialists are required, and how the story of the victim should be related to these observations. Today, doctors and human rights organizations around the world widely refer to the Istanbul Protocol to detect the physical and psychological signs of torture.[19]

In the contested human rights history of Turkey, the first decade of the 2000s is usually defined as relatively peaceful years in which the state officials took concrete steps to meet the EU accession requirements in the field of human rights. For example, it is during this period that human rights trainings were given to state officials including police officers (Babül 2017). The Kurdish guerrilla organization PKK declared a unilateral ceasefire in 1999. The peaceful atmosphere in the Kurdish region, in a sense, allowed the state to adopt a more liberal approach toward human rights issues. In this context of a relatively visible state support for human rights, the CFM submitted a proposal to the EU for awareness raising and training for the Istanbul Protocol among doctors, prosecutors, and judges in 2004. The Ministry of Justice wanted to prevent these trainings on several occasions and sought to disqualify figures such as Dr. Fincancı as a trainer. In response, the Turkish Medical Association and Forensic Specialists Association withdrew from the project. After long negotiations, the trainings started as planned, with four thousand doctors and five hundred prosecutors and judges attending these training sessions in 2008 and 2009. Regardless of the practical consequences of these trainings in terms of preventing or moderating violence, they attest to the growing power of forensic fantasies among political and bureaucratic actors.

These were the years when discourses and practices surrounding torture documentation diffused into and shaped the legal and political discussions regarding the disproportionate use of police force. However, these were also the years when older forms of state violence slowly disappeared, making it difficult to locate where the proportionate use of police force ends and torture begins.

Blurring Boundaries of Torture

The close ties between doctors and victims of political violence within the foundation enabled the former to observe how torture techniques changed over the years. The kidnapping of subversives and torturing them to death in clandestine or official detention centers was prevalent in the 1980s and 1990s. Secret rooms in police stations, hidden detention centers, and captivity sites were places where extreme forms of torture were exercised on the bodies of dissidents. These were public secrets, known to people without necessarily being witnessed or observed. In those years, there was a tendency to invisibilize torture as a state tactic, and doctors positioned themselves as actors who were uncovering the truth of violence despite the government's efforts to hide it. These doctors asked if the tortured bodies could become proof of state violence, effectively canceling the possibility of denial in the legal sphere (see Chapter 1).

Compiling data from the applicants as well as torture-related news on national and local media, the foundation's archive on torture suggests that forms of state violence were changing in the first half of the 2000s. As a recent publication by the Human Rights Foundation of Turkey summarizing the historical trajectory of the changes in forms of torture notes, classical forms of torture such as falanga and Palestinian hanging were replaced by "torture in the street."[20] That is to say, "Violence and torture are becoming widespread and turning into an almost collective and ordinary experience both for the perpetrators and the victims." The then head of the Human Rights Foundation of Turkey, Dr. Fincancı, explained this transformation further in one of our interviews: "The crime of torture can be committed on the streets; you don't have to have special torture methods for torture to occur. Today, the most common type of torture is beating. It is now being committed on the streets, within police cars, and in abandoned places in daylight."

That the police no longer used special interrogation techniques in police stations or in clandestine spaces had consequences for torture documentation and forensic fantasies. My interviews with the doctors in different branches of foundation revealed that even the victims of torture had trouble naming their experiences as torture. To address this problem, doctors made sure to rephrase their questions about torture while recording the stories of applicants during medical examinations. Dr. Gizem has been working as a part-time doctor for fifteen years at the foundation. During one of our interviews, she mentioned the risks and limitations of using the term torture during these examinations in recent years. As she said: "In many situations, the applicants don't count beating or being slapped on the face as police violence or torture. They do not even mention these. So we ask the applicant if the police officer has beaten, slapped, or hit them, or if he cursed at them, sexually harassed them, and so on. You have to name all those different kinds of violence so that he or she can discuss them. Torture is such an abstract and extreme term for them."

Doctors at the Human Rights Foundation of Turkey often mentioned how the increased use of the term "excessive use of force" (aşırı güç kullanımı) instead of "torture" in the media implicitly legitimizes the widespread use of violence by security forces during mass protests. There has emerged an ambiguous demarcation between the "excessive use of riot control agents" and their being used as torture weapons by the police. These doctors wanted to expand the boundaries of the definition of torture by telling the applicants that "disproportionate use of force" amounted to torture. When I asked Dr. Gizem to tell me more about these forms of torture, she said:

> Today, the most widespread method is beating. They kick, punch, and slap people, and they use batons, walkie-talkies, and rifle butts or handles to hit a person. Rear-handcuffing has become the norm, even though it is actually a method of torture. There are also arbitrary practices, such as not allowing people to go to the toilet. For example, if a person is on a hunger strike, they do not give them the water-salt-sugar mixture that their lawyer brought. For the rest of the detainees, they provide very little and poor-quality food. They keep people under extremely unhygienic conditions where there is no window. They also keep the light on all night long, causing people to lose track of time.

The primary purpose of the contemporary forms of torture, she maintained, was no longer to get information or confession but rather to destroy the willpower of the detainee or protestor, to make them feel unimportant and to depersonalize them. Despite their damaging consequences on the body and soul, these forms of violence were not considered torture in the public imagination, and that's what the doctors now had to struggle with as the police forces adopted new tactics and public discourses in renaming torture as something that was not torture.

To draw attention to the shifting terrain of torture and its implications for the human rights struggle, the doctors at the foundation frequently tell this story: imagine a group of protestors surrounded by the police. It is not necessary to use force on these people. If the police use pepper gas on these people who are already surrounded and controlled by the police, this is nothing but torture. But in practice, it is hard to maintain the argument in this story as the encounters between protestors and the police are much more complicated. First of all, the police are very likely to argue that they use force because the protestors resist (Feldman 1994). Therefore, they insist that it is a necessary level of force that they exert on protestors. Second, in case people get seriously hurt by the police during these encounters, it is now very common that the police do not take them into custody so that they do not go through a mandatory medical examination at a hospital. Finally, these beatings usually do not leave long-term scars on the body. This means that it is even more difficult to prove them.

Doctors at the foundation therefore wanted to expand the public definition and understanding of torture by showing how most of the beatings in the street by the police should be considered torture. The most recent research project of Dr. Fincancı initiated right before she retired from her position as a professor of forensic medicine at university exemplifies the doctors' position. Observing that torture has now spilled onto the streets through police beatings and replaced old forms of torture such as falanga or Palestinian hanging, Dr. Fincancı and her research team wanted to devise a technique to prove police beatings even after the bodily bruises disappear. They figured that they could use infrared thermal cameras to understand if there was a temperature change in the tissue under the beaten body part even after bruises disappear. They hoped that this research would give them the opportunity to write medical reports that scientifically proved whether a person was subjected to police brutality through beatings. The question for doctors invested in forensic fantasies has then in recent years boiled down to whether they could develop techniques to prove torture in the form of mundane police violence in a context of increasingly ambiguous boundaries.

What Forensic Fantasy Makes Invisible

Forensic fantasies appeal to the doctors who are involved in human rights work as they could project a unique political subjectivity through a desire to discover what is structurally hidden. The repeated scenes and scenarios about finding out the truth of state violence with the help of medical knowledge is their political commentary about the operation of power and violence in modern societies. The narratives of these doctors tend to emphasize the linear continuity of their struggles instead of ruptures or breaks thanks to forensic fantasies, which "enable individuals and groups to give themselves histories" (Scott 2012, 51). They construct their personal and collective histories by imposing "sequential order on otherwise chaotic and contingent occurrences," (Scott 2012, 51) that is, by telling a continuous and progressive narrative regarding the impact of their torture-documentation practices. Doctors' progressive narratives feed on the dialectical relationship between human rights activists who want to prove violence and state officials who want to hide or deny evidence of torture. This bears the risk of producing a very specific and narrow understanding of violence, a unique truth regime centering on the suffering body as if forensic documents are the only available way of producing knowledge about violence. Doctors' discourses draw our attention to the tortured bodies of these people, distancing us from questions such as who these people are, on what grounds they were detained and arrested, through what mechanisms and relationships their case goes public, and whether their case is kept on the national agenda or not. This chapter points to the importance of forensic fantasy in mobilizing doctors as political actors and the limitations of human rights historiography this fantasy breeds. This does not mean to discredit the human rights work of doctors. On the contrary, my purpose is to deepen our understanding of the doctors' movement in relation to the human rights movement and the broader political transformations in the country by historicizing the forensic fantasy.

Once the primary target of doctors' politics is the determination of the bodily and psychological consequences of undue state violence, their discourses and practices—inspired by forensic fantasies—inevitably target the state, address the state, and negotiate with the state. In other words, the dialectics of proof and fantasy of human rights violations are so strong that they make us forget the fact that it is these violations that underpin the legal framework in the first place (Bargu 2014a). As doctors were drawn to legal and juridical field, all other relationships, networks, and infrastructures that sustain human rights struggles might remain in the dark. As we have shown above, it is through the testimonial struggles of torture survivors at the sites of human rights institutions that doctors were able to produce forensic manuals, protocols, and reports about people's torture experiences. If the state had not invested forensic medicine with such authority (Chapter 1), and if the survivors had not produced narratives and established material links and connections with doctors, these developments that doctors narrate proudly could probably not have taken place. Against the backdrop of a historical perspective on the formation of these forensic fantasies, how they are sustained, and with what consequences, in the next chapter I examine the everyday life of forensic fantasy by centering the experiences of doctors who are employed by the state and required by law to document scars of torture.

CHAPTER 3

The Everyday Work of Keeping
the Forensic Fantasy Alive

The police stopped two Kurdish brothers on their way home for iftar (Ramadan dinner) in Istanbul on August 4, 2012, suspecting that they had carried and used drugs. After conducting a routine body search, a police officer told one of the brothers to take off his pants. The brother proposed going to a café or another enclosed place so that he would not be exposed in the middle of the street in broad daylight. However, the police officer did not accept his proposition. The other brother, who witnessed the scene, had a mild intellectual disability.[1] He shouted at the police officer who frisked his brother. In the end, the brothers were taken into custody. In the application to the prosecutor's office that the brothers eventually filed, they claimed to have been continuously beaten first in the police car, then in front of the police station, and finally inside the police station. Half an hour after they were taken into custody, an ambulance was called to take them to the hospital, as their condition deteriorated. Having been informed about the incident, their family rushed to the hospital, but they were not allowed to see the brothers.

The police and the hospital's security personnel assaulted the family members (the mother and two other brothers) when they insisted on seeing their detained relatives. After a police officer hit the mother, her two other sons attacked the police in retaliation. The cameras in the hospital's emergency department recorded the fight, and it is through these recordings that the public learned of the incident. The footage that was leaked to a TV station was two minutes long and did not provide any contextual information regarding previous incidents. Moreover, while broadcasting the event, all TV channels used the same headline: "Brutality Against the Police at the Hospital."[2] The news reports even declared that the family members were violent drug dealers.

The brothers were later taken to two different hospitals to receive mandatory medical reports. In the first hospital, the police officers insisted on entering the examination room despite the protocol that ensured doctor-patient confidentiality. The doctor refused to examine the patient and issue a medical report under these circumstances. The police officers therefore took the detainees to another hospital, where the protocol was breached as well. Despite the police presence in the examination area, the doctor on duty in the second hospital examined the brothers and documented their bruises, scars, and pain. According to the medical report issued that night, one of the brothers' eyes were seriously injured as a result of the police beating. Subsequently, he underwent two surgeries and ended up with a 50 percent vision loss.

About three weeks later, on August 22, 2012, I met this family at the office of the Human Rights Association in Istanbul. The place was packed with journalists and human rights activists. There was going to be a press release[3] about the incident. The family wanted to inform the public that the police had threatened them not to disclose anything about the torture the brothers had experienced on August 4.[4] Scars and bruises were still visible on their faces. During the press release, the brothers showed the medical reports they had received from the hospital, as a proof of the violence they had been subjected to. Ironically, the police involved in the beating of the two brothers and their family had also filed a lawsuit against the family and claimed that the brothers "had resisted and hit the police officers on duty." Just like the brothers, the police officers had received medical reports showing their injuries, which they would use in court. In other words, each party claimed to have been assaulted and injured on the basis of the reports they had received in different medical institutions. One immediately recognizes three means whereby the factuality of the "violence" during the incident was claimed, publicized, and recognized: 1) the testimony of the people directly involved in the incident (be it the police or the family), 2) the video footage, and 3) the medical reports. However, the legal proceedings and public controversies around this case often boiled down to what the medical reports said.

Medical reports prepared for legal purposes (also known as forensic reports, or *adli raporlar* in Turkish) have gained unprecedented importance beginning in the early 2000s in establishing the plausibility or implausibility of police brutality either in court, the popular discourse, or the media. For example, İsmail Saymaz (2012), a reporter who specializes in human rights violations in Turkey, picks his cases based on whether the victim of police violence received a medical report immediately after torture, beating, or ill-treatment. As he writes in the introduction to his book, *Zero Tolerance When Fallen into the Hands of the Police* (Polisin Eline Düşünce Sıfır Tolerans), having a medical report is the most solid evidence that establishes the factuality of an event. That is why police officers, aware of the importance of medical reports also seek to receive medical reports documenting their scars and injuries that might have occurred at the time of the incident.[5] This is a precautionary tactic in case they are accused of perpetrating undue violence.

The idea that medical reports are the undeniable "evidence" of police violence is powerful in the public imagination. As shown in the previous chapter, doctors' systematic and dedicated investment in forensic fantasies in human rights organizations, clinics, and hospitals to fight torture continued throughout the 1990s and played an important role in cultivating this public imagination. These were also the years when the government was dealing with internal and external pressures for its violation of human rights. Political parties used human rights in their political campaigns, promised to institute the Ministry of Human Rights, or issued official regulations to end torture. To release pressure and substantiate the claim that they were taking necessary measures to prevent torture, the government introduced a novel regulation as part of the amendments in the "Regulation on Apprehension, Detention and Statement Taking" ("Yakalama, Gözaltına Alma ve İfade Alma Yönetmeliği") in 1998.[6] Article 9 of the regulation, namely mandatory medical examinations of detainees, established that medical reports should be prepared on admission to, any prolongation of, and exit from police custody and stipulated that copies of medical reports be sent by the doctor in a sealed envelope to the prosecutor.[7] With this regulation, the state actors introduced a self-surveillance mechanism to protect the principle of habeas corpus with the help of doctors in state hospitals. No one could be officially taken into custody without a forensic report issued by a doctor working in a public hospital. No one could be released from custody without a report. This legally mandated practice was aimed at detecting whether torture and ill-treatment occurred in custody. As the opening story to this chapter exemplifies, the police had to take detainees to a public hospital before and after detention to get medical certificates regarding their well-being. The everyday reality of police violence now implicitly indexed the phantasmal promise that torture in custody could be detected with examinations before and after detention.

The right to medical examination is in line with a biopolitical paradigm in modern societies that binds the state to ensure the physical presence of a person in court. This regulation has also brought the question of forensic documentation to the center of any interaction with the police in Turkey, paving the way for a comprehensive "body-evidence regime" (Maguire and Rao 2018, 11). In practice, this regulation meant an explosion of encounters among the police, doctors, and detainees through the mediation of a phantasmal promise of the law. The belief in the power of the medical gaze in detecting torture traces on the body through a bureaucratic and legal mechanism suggests that there is an official expectation that doctors in public hospitals can document torture.

This phantasm-induced legal reform has created a routine and massive exchanges between police stations and public hospitals while transferring detainees back and forth. Everyday these exchanges produce contentious encounters between the police as "force experts" (Akarsu 2024) with legal authority to use force and doctors as official medical experts obligated to detect the use of force. These routine bureaucratic encounters encapsulate diverse priorities of different state officials and legal regulations regarding how the bodies under state care should be treated. There are inconsistencies in regulations and instructions regarding the rights and obligations of doctors and the police vis-à-vis detainees, prisoners, and each other.

Despite the universal conventions and domestic regulations that protect doctor-patient privilege, some domestic regulations give the security forces the right to compromise this privilege. One such regulation is the Trilateral Protocol, which was signed by the Ministry of Health, the Ministry of Internal Affairs, and the Ministry of Justice in 2003 to regulate health examinations of prisoners in hospitals.[8] The protocol explicitly states that the law enforcement officers can enter an examination room where the prisoner will be examined if the windows have no iron bars. Rather than requiring the security forces, prosecutor, or hospital administration to build a safe area or room with iron bars for detainees or prisoners who visit the hospital, the Trilateral Protocol allows the security forces to be present during the examination. Even though the Health Control Article 9 explicitly states that the examination should ensure the doctor-patient privilege, some law enforcement officers insist on staying in the room by referring to the Trilateral Protocol. Because of these contradictory regulations on the rights and responsibilities of the security forces, a degree of contention and arbitrariness are embedded in the implementation of this article.

A similar ambiguity pertains to the interpretation of doctors' roles and rights in these encounters. Occupying the margins of state bureaucracy, these emergency-ward doctors work at state hospitals and produce official documents in the name of the state through micro encounters with the police and detainees. However, these doctors are far from representing a unified or homogenous group; on the contrary, they are extremely diverse in terms of their training, political background, age, and gender. Some of them are interns working in the emergency ward temporarily. Others are emergency medicine or forensic medicine specialists. The doctors' approach to this mandatory practice varies depending on their political views, professional background, and competence in preparing forensic reports. While some of them refuse to examine the patient in the presence of security officers, others see no other option but to examine the patient.

During my research in four different hospitals in several neighborhoods of Istanbul, I observed great diversity in encounters among doctors, security forces, and detainees during the detainee examinations. The institutional culture of the hospital, the material infrastructure of the clinic, and one's personal convictions shape how doctors examine the patient in a way to solidify or weaken one's investment in forensic fantasies. As we have discussed earlier, fantasies are used as analytics to understand the constitution of the sociality of national community (Hage 2000) and the role of political imaginations in the formation of the reality of the state (Rose 1996; Aretxaga 2003; Taussig 1997). Rather than opposing fantasy and reality, these studies highlighted how fantasies, alongside passions, intimacies, and attachments, enable social and political reality. The analytics of fantasy was also used to analyze social movements (Morris 2022), political activists (Hermez 2015), consumer practices (Patel 2007), and citizenship formations (Navaro-Yashin 2012). All these studies show that people's attachments to certain fantasies link them to broader communities, shaping their expectations and aspirations for the future. Examining the routine clinical examination of detainee's health through the lens of forensic fantasy gives us insights into the constitution of professional expert identity vis-à-vis the workings of the state. This especially applies to doctors who are producing these routine forensic reports in public hospitals.

After providing the historical trajectory of this mandatory health-examination requirement and highlighting how progressive narratives surrounding this article has been constitutive of forensic fantasies around this article, namely the belief that torture in custody can be detected and restricted, I demonstrate that even though

certain types of narratives are essential to maintain forensic fantasies, it is through practical involvement that doctors keep themselves
committed to this fantasy. Doctors' varying degrees of attachment to
this fantasy are most visible in the narratives, stories, objects, and
encounters that circulate during the examination of the detainee/
patient in the clinic for the purposes of report production. Keeping
the forensic fantasy alive has two main dimensions: doctors' daily
work at the workplace and their regular engagement with similar-
minded doctors in non-clinical spaces. It is through the daily forensic practices at the hospital that doctors invest in professional expert
identity as well as the idea of the state.

The Narrative Construction of Legally
Sanctioned Forensic Fantasies

I first learned about doctors' debates on this mandatory examination
regulation in 2008. Within the scope of Turkey's EU accession process, the government organized a series of human rights trainings for
state officials. I specifically followed trainings on the Istanbul Protocol,[9] which aimed to train participants about the medical, legal, and
ethical norms and regulations regarding medical documentation of
torture and ill-treatment. Doctors, police officers, and prosecutors
were the attendees. Yet, these trainings primarily targeted doctors
who worked in state hospitals and issued mandatory medical reports
regarding detainees' well-being as part of their daily routines. Trainings included details about how doctors could undertake a forensic
examination of detainees in line with the principles of the Istanbul
Protocol as well as national regulations.[10] While I was listening to the
presentations of the training doctors, I was struck by their optimistic stance toward doctors' capabilities to restrict police violence. The
trainers argued that doctors in state hospitals had a responsibility
to mobilize their medical-expert knowledge in the name of medical
ethics. It was also their responsibility to prevent security officers from
entering the examination room in accordance with the stipulations in

international and national documents. In short, the trainers conveyed to their diverse audience the following message: If implemented properly, this regulation could end or at least restrict police brutality. If not, doctors could be found guilty afterward because of the medical ethics that required doctors to say "no" to the police when they wanted to enter the examination room. If one did not comply with the principles of medical ethics while implementing this regulation, their actions would be legally punishable.

These trainers' intensely affective engagement with this regulation is inseparable from their broader political project of creating a society free of torture with the help of documentation. One of these doctors was Dr. Elmas, who was working as a forensic doctor in one of the branches of the CFM. Identifying as a leftist, she has been active in various social movements since the 1970s and continues to advocate for human and women's rights, frequently speaking at panels, conferences, and protests. We started our interview in a dark and stuffy room in a small courthouse where she worked as an official senior forensic expert on legal cases sent by prosecutors. At the time of our interview, she was no longer conducting mandatory examinations of detainees as she used to do in the 1990s. When I asked her to describe the circumstances at the beginning of her career as a forensic expert, she told me about an intimidating encounter with the police chief who had worked in a nearby station back then. The encounter had taken place in Dr. Elmas's office in a small courthouse located in a poor and distant Istanbul neighborhood. Ever since her first day on the job as a forensic doctor, she realized that all detainees brought from a nearby police station to receive pre- and post-detention examination reports were tortured. Coming from a leftist background, she had sympathies for all marginalized and oppressed social groups such as radical leftists, Kurdish activists, sex workers, street children, and the homeless who were more likely to be subjected to police violence. Despite her good intentions, she failed to document torture most of the time because detainees, fearful that torture might continue when they went back to the police station, could not tell her about the torture they had undergone. However, her sympathy toward torture victims bothered police officers. One day the chief of a nearby police station dropped by her office unexpectedly. Having pulled his gun out and put it on her desk, he said: "Your door might be knocked and people you don't know can rape you. In case such a thing happens—I want you to know that—we would do everything in our power to defend you." She told me how helpless and vulnerable she felt as a young woman doctor after hearing the implied threat coming from a police chief: "We cannot even compare today's cases to what was happening back then. They tortured every single detainee. The police were so powerful. For example, we would carbon copy the reports and give them to the police so they could deliver them to relevant authorities. Yet, they would take these reports and tear them apart in front of our eyes if they did not like their content. We were not able to do anything."

According to Dr. Elmas, back then the police had nothing to fear and wanted to prevent torture documentation and intimidate doctors willing to document torture. Dr. Elmas's story and other similar accounts where doctors were either explicitly or implicitly threated by the police during the detainee examinations are often told in human rights trainings and trauma conferences organized by doctors who dedicate themselves to torture documentation. For example, during a training workshop for forensic doctors organized by the Society of Forensic Medicine Specialists, Dr. Mehmet, a professor of forensic medicine and a well-known forensic expert on human rights violations, was giving a presentation on the importance of implementing the principles of the Istanbul Protocol in detainee examinations. In the middle of his presentation, he turned to the doctors in the audience, who had come to the training from public hospitals all around Turkey, and asked them to recall any significant progress they had made over the years as forensic doctors. After telling the audience Dr. Elmas's story, he added that doctors had been afraid to ask for a separate examination room or conduct a full-body examination because they felt powerless in the police presence. "But now," he emphasized, "we have a standard thanks to the Istanbul Protocol. We have made progress. It is our success and our responsibility to protect it."

The notion of progressive gain is a theme that consistently comes up in the narratives of doctors who have been politically active in the field of torture documentation and human rights. Older generations of forensic doctors used every opportunity to emphasize the progress made in the field of torture documentation and the importance of protecting these legal gains. This emphasis persisted well after the first decade of the 2000s, a period that is now nostalgically remembered as the EU years. For example, during our interview, Dr. Fincancı, who is known for her scientific and political contributions to the field of torture documentation, told the story of a teacher who had died of a heart attack while in custody in the aftermath of the July 15 coup attempt in 2016. According to her, his death is the first documented torture case after the coup attempt thanks to the procedural safeguards instituted into the system with their struggles. She explains: "While he was in police custody, he was taken to the hospital and examined by a doctor every twenty-four hours. Some of the doctors he saw while in custody recorded his story and documented his wounds and bruises in detail thanks to procedural safeguards, especially article 9 on health control." Doctors at the CFM also prepared a detailed and qualified autopsy report after his death. Analyzing mandatory medical-examination reports and his autopsy report in detail, Dr. Fincancı and her friends established that the teacher, already a diabetic patient, had been denied access to his insulin and treated badly. Fincancı says: "When we compiled all those data,[11] we could say that that young man wouldn't have died if he hadn't been treated that way." Then, drawing on the accumulated evidence, Dr. Fincancı says they concluded that although the teacher's death had not taken place during or right after the beating while in custody, there was a connection between his death and conditions he had been subjected to, namely the circumstances of his custody. These safeguards, resulting from doctors' years-long struggles, helped them explain this connection scientifically and argue that his death had been caused by the bad treatment he had been subjected to.

There has been political turmoil and systematic backlash against the procedural guarantees in the country in the last decade, together with the radical decline of the legitimacy of human rights discourses. Yet, these senior doctors continue to underline the importance of holding up to the principles of the Istanbul Protocol during the clinical examination of detainees in seminars, trainings, panels, and conferences. Their progressive narrative erases the incoherence and conflict surrounding the history and implementation of this regulation, while emphasizing doctors' agency in creating the conditions under which detainee examinations could be conducted properly. Radical interpretation of legal regulations given by these doctors is often far from representing the reality of detainee examinations in hospitals. Doctors in public hospitals who deal with medical-report requests from the police complain about the difficulty of implementing the Istanbul Protocol, as suggested during the trainings. For example, whether police officers can enter the examination room depends on many factors such as the existence of a secure examination room in the hospital, the attitude of hospital administration and the police toward the detainee, and the broader political atmosphere regarding detention procedures. These doctors cite insufficient hospital infrastructures, rude and dominating attitude of the police, and detainees' reluctance to give consent to a full-body examination. Doctors' diverse approaches to these clinical examinations of detainees depend on the level of their investment in forensic fantasies. Against all odds, these progressive narratives continue to shape the perception of forensic doctors who are invested in these fantasies and determined to detect human rights violations. Investing in these forensic fantasies is possible only through the daily practical work of doctors amid the bureaucratic difficulties.

The Everyday Work of Keeping
the Forensic Fantasy Alive

Senior forensic doctors who devoted themselves to documenting torture inspired a generation of medical students to believe in the power of medicine in detecting human rights violations. When these students became doctors and started to work in state hospitals, they took up the challenge of creating an ideal examination environment to keep this fantasy alive in their daily encounters with detainees and the police. Dr. Okan was working as a forensic specialist in a training and research hospital in Istanbul at the time of my research. He decided to specialize in forensic medicine after taking a class with Dr. Şebnem Korur Fincancı during his training at the medical school. Inspired by her human rights–centered approach to forensic medicine, he developed an understanding that views the principles of medical ethics and human rights as compatible with each another. I met Dr. Okan in a human rights training workshop. He invited me to the forensic clinic he was working at to see with my own eyes how mandatory medical examinations were conducted. The clinic he invited me to was a one-story building next to the emergency ward of a public hospital. When he was appointed as the head specialist in the forensic medicine outpatient clinic in this hospital, Dr. Okan wanted to move forensic medical practice out of the emergency ward. He proposed introducing a forensic-documentation system that would produce truthful and scientific medical documents about detainees' health, and he would need a new building dedicated to forensic examinations. Dr. Okan lobbied for the building of this separate unit in the hospital for more than a year, and to his surprise, the chief physician's office finally supported the project and raised money for the construction of a separate clinic for forensic medicine. When I asked him what the reporting system was like when he first started working there, he told me how furious he'd been to see doctors conducting forensic examinations in the hospital:

> There was a doctor who examined the detainee or patient from his seat while smoking in a small examination room in the emergency ward. The policemen could easily enter the room. The doctor had a stamp in his hand that read "no signs of battery or violence detected" [*darb ve cebir izi yoktur*], which he used in reports without examining the patient. When I first entered the room and saw the stamp

on his desk, I got so angry that I threw it out. I was determined to ensure that regulations were going to be truthfully implemented, and I never backed down from this stance. Dealing with these issues requires a strong background in human rights.

Dr. Okan was angry because the practice of reporting in the hospital was not in line with the requirements of the relevant regulations, yet he was equally motivated to create proper conditions for the medical examination of detainees. When I first went there, I saw many police officers and detainees in the waiting area. I hesitated to enter the examination room, suspecting that there might be a patient inside. Instead, I called the doctor on his cell phone. He met me outside the waiting area and walked me into the examination room, passing by the police officers and detainees. In the examination room, there was a bed behind a screen and a desk for the medical secretary, who was a young man wearing a jacket and a tie and typing on a computer. The doctor introduced me to him and showed me his own room, which could be accessed directly from the examination room. Inside the room, there was a desk and a small kitchen. He used this room to take short breaks from his busy schedule.

In the following months, I spent hours in Dr. Okan's office, chatting with him about his work at the clinic. I also talked to two other doctors and the medical secretary at the clinic. Our conversations were frequently interrupted by new examination requests, as this was one of the busiest forensic clinics in Istanbul. There was a constant circulation of detainees between two police officers coming and going to the clinic. Doctors there worked in shifts and saw approximately 50 people a day, or 1,500 people a month. Since they prepared two reports for a single applicant (entry and exit reports),[12] they were preparing more than fifty thousand reports every year. Despite his busy schedule, Dr. Okan usually sounded happy and proud when he talked about the forensic-documentation system he had established there.

During our conversations in his small room at the back of the examination area, Dr. Okan recounted many stories that revolved around his interactions with the police. I realized that a somewhat pedagogical approach and political distance underscored his attitude toward the police. Once, as I was waiting in his room, he came back from examining a detainee and asked me if I had overheard the dialogue he'd had with the police officer at the door. I did not. Dr. Okan had joked with one of them for the first time since he started to work there. The police officer was surprised. "I've been coming here for two years," he said, "and this is the first time I see you like this i.e. joking and smiling, doctor." "One should be very careful when talking to the police," Dr. Okan added. When I asked him to elaborate, he said: "Here, you should always keep the police at a distance. If you say, 'what's up, dude, or how are you?' to a police officer, you send a wrong message to the patient/detainee." According to Dr. Okan, "What you're doing is potentially against the police. But when you engage in a dialogue with the police, you cannot build trust with the patient." To him, not letting one's guard down was the most important thing. Forensic doctors should physically and emotionally remain distant from the police. That is why, he often says, "I always walk around with a [metaphorical] mask on here." He sounded especially proud when he said he had never entered into a dialogue with the police except for a very few greetings.

When he had started to work at that hospital, the first thing he wanted to do was to teach the police officers to wait in front of the examination room. Previously the police had thought they were entitled to enter the examination room with the detainee and watch the doctor examine the patient and write their report. To prevent this, he printed out Article 6, which regulated medical examinations, and put it up on the walls of the clinic. The police gradually accepted the order he had established in the clinic. Dr. Okan had indeed founded a system that minimized his interactions with the police. He always kept his office door locked so the police could not enter his room from the second door opening to the waiting area. The arriving police officers typically gave the secretary a letter of request with the detainee's name. The secretary would put their name on a list. Dr. Okan then called the patients from the list, one by one, reading out the names in the waiting area. Once I was waiting for the doctor with five police officers in the waiting area. When a detainee's name was called out, the police officer who brought him tried to enter the examination room with the detainee, but the other police officers warned him that "this doctor doesn't let us in." Apparently, as it was his first time in this clinic, he did not know the rules. A sturdy, tall man, Dr. Okan would stand by the door and physically stop the police officers who wanted to enter the examination room. Most police officers already knew that they were not allowed in the examination room and agreed to wait in front of the room till the end of the examination, without making a fuss about it. In sum, Dr. Okan's hard-earned system was working with his determination and keeping the forensic fantasy alive for him.

Another doctor that I visited was Dr. Eren. She worked as a forensic doctor in the emergency ward of a public hospital as well. She was given a small room titled "forensic examinations." Also trained by Dr. Şebnem Korur Fincancı at the medical school, she was affectively invested in the idea of forensic documentation of human rights violations and had even worked as a volunteer forensic doctor at the Human Rights Foundation of Turkey for two years, where she prepared medical certificates for torture victims. She was excited and surprised when she learned about her appointment as a forensic doctor in one of the most populous hospitals in Istanbul. She knew that that hospital was notorious for its complicity with the police as the latter could easily enter doctors' offices and put pressure on them to get the kind of medical reports they wanted.

Dr. Eren worked in a narrow room close to the hospital's emergency entrance. Like Dr. Okan, she was determined to examine the detainees properly and write detailed and truthful forensic reports regarding their health. Her narrative about her work revolved around her struggles to convince police officers to uncuff the detainees. She also developed various strategies to keep the police outside the examination room if they insisted on entering. For example, she sometimes acted as if the situation were out of her control, saying: "There is nothing I can do about it. These are the rules and there are cameras everywhere. If I let you in, they can file a complaint against me." At other times, she tried to calm the police officers by ensuring them that the detainee could not escape from the room or hurt her: "The room is secure. There are iron bars on the windows. There is a male secretary inside and you'll be right outside in case of emergency. Nothing in the room can be used to hurt people." Keeping the police away from the examination room was a challenging task for this young woman doctor given the insistence of the police officers in that hospital. The police are powerful in these encounters not only because they carry guns but also because they are familiar with the whole process. They want to have these medical certificates as quickly as possible so that they could start the official detention process or release the detainee. The police can also be anxious during these encounters, as they know that these medical reports can be used as evidence to file a suit against them if the doctor reports an act of disproportionate use of force. Therefore, a forensic report that truthfully documents torture might restrict the violence of the perpetrator. The fantasy that medical expertise will produce evidence against state violence informs these doctors' encounters with the police. The construction of a cold distance from the police in the clinic keeps the fantasy alive for these experts.

These doctors experience problems not only with the police but also with the detainees who are most of the time not knowledgeable about these reports and tend to see the examinations as yet another bureaucratic nuisance they were subjected to while in custody. The encounters with detainees in Dr. Okan's clinic usually unfold as follows: He reads out the name of the detainee he is going to examine, and the police bring him in. Dr. Okan stops the police at the door and asks them to uncuff the detainee before the examination. He never examines a patient in handcuffs. During the examination, the doctor asks a detainee to take off his clothes to see if there is ecchymosis and abrasion on the body. Then he asks the patient to stretch his arms forward and turn around. He listens to his lungs with his stethoscope and always asks: "Have you been subjected to any sort of ill-treatment and torture in custody?" Most of the time the answer is no. Some detainees even add, "Never, the police were very good to me. I'm grateful," as if the police were still around, observing them. For many detainees, as it is for the police, this hospital visit is a burden that they want to unload as soon as possible.

The torture methods of the 1990s such as falanga or electric shock still haunt most people when they imagine what torture looks like. That is why, Dr. Okan explains, even in cases when the detainees were badly beaten, they deny any torture. He always asks more specific questions that might help detainees describe their current state of health such as: "How are you feeling right now? Do you have any complaints? Do you have any health problems? Are you currently taking any medicine? Do you have the medicine now?" Depending on the detainee's response, he asks more questions to help them elaborate. In case the detainee does not have access to their medicine or if they suffer from a chronic disease that requires medical attention, Dr. Okan would ask the police to take the detainee to the emergency ward for further consultation. In some cases, the detainee would say: "I don't have any complaints and I don't want to take off my clothes for examination." In such cases, Dr. Okan responds: "I can examine you only if you take your clothes off. But you have the right not to be examined. In that case, I have to write that down and get your signature." Dr. Okan never prepares a health report without conducting a full-body examination of the patient because it is the only way to do a proper medical examination and document police violence. Dr. Eren has a similar approach to these examinations. After inquiring about detainees' general health, she would ask if they had any physical complaint at that moment and if they had been subjected to any ill-treatment while being taken into custody or during their time in police custody. If their answer is negative, she asks if there were any other bruises or scars that might have occurred earlier. She tells the detainees that she will examine them and note any scars that were on their bodies. She is particularly keen on detailing the detainees' stories before the examinations.

Inspired and trained by Dr. Fincancı, both doctors are determined to detect traces of state violence on detainees' bodies. They are optimistic about the power of documentation despite structural problems they encounter. Overcoming these problems requires a lot of work in their engagements with other doctors, the police, and detainees. Their investment in the phantasmal promise that a torture-free society is possible is also constitutive of their professional and political identities as forensic experts. They act as if the full realization of this fantasy were possible only in so far as they actively seek ways of getting rid of technical and practical problems that would prevent proper forensic examination. Yet, they are aware that a proper examination cannot be conducted under the current conditions. For example, Dr. Eren says:

> It is almost impossible to create an ideal examination environment. I sometimes feel desperate, knowing that detainees will return to police custody after the examination. The torture might continue regardless. You feel that you have to be careful about what you write. Also, even though you know that a thorough examination requires more time, you cannot prolong it as there are other patients or detainees waiting outside. You have to cut it short. Detainees usually wait for their examination in stuffy police buses, and I know that if I do not shorten the examination period, the police might decide to take the detainees to another hospital where doctors might not even bother to examine them at all.

Even though she does her best to prepare accurate reports, she does not work at the hospital 24/7. "Sometimes I realize there are baton marks on a detainee's back," she says. "But when I check the entry report prepared the previous night [i.e., when she was not at work], it is not mentioned. Some doctors don't even bother to ask detainees to take their clothes off." Despite these disillusionments and moments of low job satisfaction, these forensic doctors do their best to implement the principles of this regulation and the Istanbul Protocol in every single encounter with police officers and detainees.

What transforms their tiresome encounters and repetitive tasks into an optimistic determination is their professional networking and their connections with colleagues, which keep them excited about their work and sustain the fantasy. These doctors regularly engage in dialogues about the mandatory examinations, their importance, and flaws and challenges in panel discussions, workshops, conferences, and vocational training courses. They affectively narrate how they incessantly try to create proper examination conditions in their everyday dialogues with other forensic doctors. It is thanks to these expert networks in non-clinical spaces that they remain invested in this fantasy. These socialites materially enable the anti-torture political mobilization of these doctors and ensure their continuous attachment to the fantasy for documentation. That is why these doctors, as hopeful experts, are motivated to get rid of practical and organizational obstacles that prevent ideal examination practices. However, not all doctors are equally invested in this fantasy. Lacking a similar level of affective intensity and engagement, this second group of doctors, which I will examine next, highlights the limitations of forensic documentation, pointing to broader structures of inequality that torture documentation fails to solve. The echoes of the fantasy are weaker in their experience. These doctors are more vocal in their cynicism vis-à-vis the work that they undertake without being deeply and affectively attached to the fantasy.

Weak Echoes of the Forensic Fantasy

When Dr. Okan moved to another city, he was concerned about the future of the documentation system he had established in the hospital. Dr. Zeynel replaced him, and despite Dr. Okan's fears, he managed to keep the system functioning. Even though Dr. Okan's system was still in place, I observed stark differences in terms of how the two doctors described their work. As a forensic doctor, Dr. Zeynel was also knowledgeable about the principles of the Istanbul Protocol and the regulation on detainee examination. However, he was not enthusiastic about the work at the clinic; on the contrary, he was critical of the human rights discourse, especially how it fixated on the acts of security forces and the question of torture and its documentation. According to him, this fixation prevented us from seeing structural inequalities against the disadvantaged groups in society. Disillusioned about the impact and import of these examinations, he said one should be concerned about the normalization of violence in our societies. When I asked him to explain his statement, he told me about his encounters with detainees during medical examinations. When he asked detainees if they had been subjected to ill-treatment in custody, some of the frequent responses he received were like this: "Not really. They [the police] just slapped me in the face" or "They just kicked me." According to him, for most people there is nothing wrong with a slap or a kick coming from the police, and this is the real problem. Doctors, in his opinion, have extremely naïve perception of violence, because, as he says: "People are subjected to violence in their daily lives. So, they don't care if the police hit them, too. They have already been beaten up, kicked in the head, dragged on the streets, abused in their families. So, people don't consider slapping or humiliation or being kept under unfavorable conditions as bad treatment or as violation of human rights. These violations are normal to them."

For him, it was doctors' naiveté that prevented them from seeing the reality. When I inquired what he meant by the "doctors naiveté," he responded: "Doctors who reduce the question of human rights to the acts of police forces towards detainees in custody." In his opinion, the notion of the human rights struggle, especially in the last quarter of the century, had been reduced to the question of torture, which was a narrow understanding of human rights. This attitude, according to him, did not do justice to the minority groups in Turkey whose language and culture were repressed, assimilated, or denied. There were different forms of inequalities in society such as gender inequality and inequalities experienced by disadvantaged groups such as the disabled, mentally ill, elderly, and poor. He even went on to include the suffering of animals in shelters, arguing that if people kept ignoring animal rights, they did not deserve a better treatment.

While Dr. Okan and Dr. Eren explained every positive practice in their clinic with reference to their determination to implement the rules and principles of examining a detainee properly, for Dr. Zeynel, the effectiveness of his documentation practice depended on institutional and infrastructural factors. Although doctors had to keep the police outside the examination room to maintain the confidentiality of medical examination, most examinations in other hospitals were performed in the presence of security forces. For him, this was expected because most police officers, whom he called "police friends" (*polis arkadaşlar*), were concerned that a detainee might escape from the examination room. Thus, they were right to insist on being present during the examination. Unless doctors have proper rooms with one entrance and secured windows, they cannot convince police officers to leave the room. Dr. Zeynel does not allow the police to enter the examination room and asks the right questions to encourage detainees to tell their stories of violence. Despite this, his approach to his job is different from Dr. Eren's or Dr. Okan's, as he is not fully invested in the forensic fantasy. He is a weak echo of the forensic fantasy we heard from Dr. Eren.[13] Here I follow Joan Scott's use of the term "echo." As an imperfect return of sound, Scott (2012) uses the analytics of fantasy echo to historically expand our horizon for the diverse possibilities of political and social identification through fantasy. By highlighting what documentation is not capable of doing, Dr. Zeynel is representing another form of identification with the forensic fantasy, suggesting the productivity of the fantasy in terms of producing a diverse range of identifications.

As I talked to more doctors in emergency-ward clinics, it became clear to me that most of them have a very weak or nonexistent relationship with the forensic fantasy. Dr. Fahri is a middle-aged emergency-ward doctor who taught himself how to do proper a forensic examination by attending trainings provided by doctors fighting for human rights. He works at a state hospital located in one of the most populous neighborhoods of Istanbul. Every day approximately seven hundred to eight hundred patients are treated in the emergency ward and at least one-tenth of these patients are there for "forensic examination" (*adli muayene*). There is no separate area for these examinations. Most reports are prepared in a corner separated by a screen in the presence of security forces. On a typical day, he asks detainees if they have any complaints or if they have any wounds and bruises. If they say "no," he says "*Geçmiş olsun*" ("Get well soon") and sends them back to police custody. This would be unacceptable practice for Dr. Okan, Dr. Eren, or Dr. Zeynel. Following the principles of the Istanbul Protocol, they refuse to write reports without conducting a full-body examination of detainee.

Dr. Fahri, however, wants to see the body only if detainees had complaints about physical abuse. Even though he is a progressive doctor knowledgeable about the Istanbul Protocol and its principles, his medical practice was shaped by infrastructural limitations such as the absence of a separate examination room for detainees and an insufficient number of medical staff to attend the patients. The hospital administration had designed a secure forensic examination room in the green area of the emergency ward. However, it is no longer in use because most emergency-ward patients are concentrated in yellow and red areas, and doctors usually do not have two minutes to walk to the room in the green area for detainee examination because the patients keep coming to the yellow area. Faced with the scarcity of doctors and the lack of a separate room in the yellow area, doctors inevitably see the patients/detainees in the middle of the emergency ward. Dr. Fahri is no exception. But he has developed his own strategy over time. If the detainee "really needs to go through the examination," Dr. Fahri asks the police officers to uncuff the patient and examines him in an injection room nearby. "This," he says, "partially meets the standards. However, most colleagues would not even bother to do this."

The police benefit from doctors' indifference toward examinations. Sometimes they do not uncuff the detainee, arguing that detainee/patient is troubled. The police might also ask doctors to examine detainees in police cars or buses, especially when seeking medical reports after the mass detention of a group of people. Because most doctors avoid getting into a debate with the police, they agree to examine patients with handcuffs on or go to the police bus for the examination of detainees. Examining patients in non-clinical spaces, especially in a police vehicle, is a strictly forbidden practice. However, many doctors, rather than challenging the police, go to the police bus and ask, "Does anyone have any complaints?" (*Şikayeti olan var mı?*). In his opinion, "No one can tell their complaints there. No one. In the middle of everyone." Therefore, Dr. Fahri feels lonely and isolated in the hospital because other doctors do not share his concerns about documentation. When he is not around or is taking care of other patients, the doctors in the clinic do whatever the police tell them to do. He always does his best to remain alone with the patient by asking police officers to stay at least behind the curtain. This is the only way to avoid doing injustice to the patient. However, he is aware that the police always search for ways to interfere with the examination, especially if excessive use of force is involved.

I once witnessed such an encounter, when the police undermined a detainee's complaints. I was in the crowded emergency ward of a public hospital that is notorious for its substandard medical reports. In front of the main entrance, there were not only ambulances but also police cars with detainees brought in for mandatory medical examination. I was with my doctor friend, who was showing me around, when a police officer and two detainees walked in the emergency ward. The police asked the triage secretary at the counter to register them. The secretary turned to the detainees and asked: "Do you have any health problems?" One of them responded: "They hit me at the back of my ears and pepper-sprayed my right eye." The police officer interrupted: "This does not count as battery." The secretary said: "If he was beaten, he has to see the doctor first." The police officer intervened again and said: "This is not battery." Then the young boy, whose hands were handcuffed behind his back, showed his wounded neck. Even I could see the redness on his neck. But the police officer insisted: "This doesn't count as battery." This went on for some time. Eventually, the police officer agreed to take the detainee inside for examination. During this encounter, the detainee, the medical secretary and the police officer tried to reach agreement on how to classify the officer's use of force. While the officer insisted that what had happened before did not count as battery (*darp*), the detainee did not take a step back. On the contrary, by showing the secretary his red neck and bruises on his ear, he made her the witness of his bodily scars. The police officer agreed to transfer him to the doctor for medical examination. We didn't have a chance to observe how the examination went and the kind of medical report that came out because the police officer and the detainee went to another corner of the emergency ward. My doctor friend, however, alerted me that what I just witnessed was an unusual moment, since the detainees would not usually complain about the beatings they were subjected to.

When they left, my friend took the old gray iron stamp from the counter and showed it to me. The stamp read: "There is no sign of battery and violence" (*Darp ve cebir izi bulunmamaktadır*). The police wanted to receive a medical document with this stamp on it. My friend said to me: "You see with your own eyes how things work here." It was my first time seeing the notorious "no sign of battery and violence" stamp that had flourished in hospitals when the government first introduced these mandatory medical examinations in 1998. Many hospitals still use them despite the complaints and campaigns for their removal during medical examinations of detainees. Signaling a bureaucratic automation of physical examination, these stamps have replaced physical examination with a ready-made statement attesting to the absence of torture and ill-treatment. Instead of physically examining the detainee, doctors or medical secretaries sometimes use this stamp after asking the detainee if they have any complaints and receive "no" as an answer.[14]

When my friend was transferred to another hospital a few years later, another forensic doctor, Dr. Selim, was appointed to this hospital. I had an interview with him as well. I first asked about the notorious stamp. It had now disappeared, but the treatment of the detainees remained the same. Dr. Selim confirmed this observation during our interview: "The police bring a detainee not as a human being, but as a thing. Most doctors do not treat detainees as patients. Even when a detainee has been heavily beaten and the police are tightly holding his arm without uncuffing him, they ask questions for the sake of asking: 'Do you have any complaints? No? OK.'" Dr. Selim found this type of treatment unacceptable.

As a newly graduated forensic doctor, Dr. Selim was working enthusiastically to transform the system. He insisted on seeing patients in a secured room. He convinced the administration to put iron bars on the windows and made sure that the police officers waited outside the room during the examination. According to him, the biggest problem was that 90 percent of the police knew nothing about the regulations. All they wanted was to "get the report as soon as possible." Dr. Selim's insistence on following the procedure soon created an uproar among the police officers who came to this hospital to get medical certificates. They spread rumors about him being a terrorist. With no respect toward Dr. Selim, once a police officer kicked the door of his office, cursing at him and his family. Finally, based on a complaint filed against him, Dr. Selim was suspended from his job right after the 2016 coup attempt. When he was acquitted and he resumed his job three months later, the situation significantly changed in the hospital because the police officers with the reputation of being violent and rude had also been suspended after the coup. However, the bureaucratic violence he experienced has changed him. He decided to take a rather hands-off approach regarding documentation as he felt supported neither by his professional association nor by human rights organizations. He felt isolated and lonely. In a bitter voice, he said he finally saw "the true colors of human rights doctors." He added that he would continue to follow the procedure, although he believed it would not make a difference.

Dr. Zeynel, Dr. Fahri, and Dr. Selim issue forensic reports at different Istanbul hospitals in line with the principles of the Istanbul

Protocol and the national regulations that protect patient-detainee privilege. However, their investment in forensic fantasy is weak and partial as they maintain that a focus on torture inevitably disregards broader structural inequalities. They do not think their individual intervention is meaningful within the broader infrastructural context where the police have the upper hand and where doctors are isolated and too busy to take care of the patient according to the regulations. It seems that enthusiastic investment in forensic fantasy is sustainable only through the communal sociality among doctors who echo each other's emotional attachment. When doctors work alone without having regular interaction with doctors engaged in a similar task, it is not possible for them to fully invest their energy in this forensic fantasy.

Regardless of how willing doctors are to implement the regulation to the letter, there are gaps in the regulation that allow the police to avoid these reports. For example, even though the law requires that the police receive these reports from a state hospital, there are no regulations specifying the hospital that should issue these reports. In many state hospitals, the police can get medical reports without doctors conducting full-body examination of detainees. That is why if police officers use disproportionate violence against detainees, they prefer to go to the hospitals known for their cursory report-writing practices. Moreover, if a doctor prepares a detailed forensic report documenting bodily scars that occurred under custody, the police can just rip up the report and take the detainee to another hospital to get other forensic reports. All in all, there are gaps in the regulation that the police can circumnavigate to avoid documentation of torture scars on a detainee's body.

In most of the hospitals I visited, there is neither a forensic doctor nor a doctor who is knowledgeable about this regulation or doctors' ethical responsibilities while examining detainees. In two of the hospitals I visited, most of the reporting is done by junior doctors. It was always challenging to arrange an interview with these doctors as they are busy and do not want to spare time on such a trivial topic like criminal examinations of detainees. When I talked to them, they made a distinction between medical treatment and reporting. These doctors are burdened with excessive workload in the emergency ward and consider both forensic examination and forensic report-writing a waste of time. Their primary job is to treat people, not to deal with forensic documentation. They are also frustrated with the fact that the police bring all detainees to the green area of the emergency ward without asking for permission. They see these examinations as a burden, especially if the person has not been subjected to violence. In other words, they want to treat those who were abused, but those who are not abused tire them. When I asked them how they conduct these examinations, Özlem, an emergency doctor, explained: "We ask the person if they have been subjected to battery. If they say 'no,' we issue a report stating that no sign of battery and violence has been detected. But if they say that battery has taken place, we take them to the yellow area, where they can be treated. In that case, forensic reports are prepared, and necessary tests and reports are requested. We assess if he is in a good enough condition to be released from the hospital or not." Indeed, in a majority of the hospitals, the police can get these medical reports without even waiting for the doctor to examine the patient. If detainees give a negative answer to the question whether they have been treated badly while in custody, most of the doctors take the detainees' word for granted and do not insist on conducting full-body examinations. They do not rephrase the question to get a more detailed answer about how detainees were treated in custody as doctors I introduced earlier would do.

Doctors' Political Subjectivities and Fantasies that Make Forensic Evidence Manifest

I do not ask whether or to what extent the mandatory health examination is effective in preventing torture, nor how the forensic reports of detainees might later be used in legal proceedings to put perpetrators on trial. By examining the everyday encounters among doctors, detainees, and the police within the clinical context,

I show that there are contradictory discursive material and relational dimensions to how doctors invest in fantasies of documentation via this regulation. What motivates certain doctors to properly implement this regulation and create an ideal examination encounter depends on their political orientation as well as the broader network of experts they are embedded in.

The progressive narratives of senior doctors who have been working in the field of human rights are key to the formation and maintenance of the forensic fantasies entailed by this regulation. These doctors are the founding expert figures in the field of forensic documentation of torture due to their background in both forensics and human rights and their ties with progressive organizations and professional associations such as the Human Rights Foundation of Turkey, the Turkish Medical Association, and the Istanbul Medical Chamber. They have created publicly available and affective narratives around this mandatory regulation, showing how its flawless implementation is the first step in the struggle against torture. By highlighting the progressive gains and the agency of doctors, these narratives not only create forensic fantasies but also inadvertently fetishize the law of the state.

This regulation implies that all doctors as official medical experts can and should document torture and become expert witnesses against state violence. However, in practice, doctors' engagement with torture documentation has proved to be complicated. I encountered two groups of doctors whose documentation practices were indexed by forensic fantasies to varying degrees. The first group of doctors realized themselves through this forensic fantasy and were taking up a more hopeful stance toward the implications of their work as they were embedded in collective professional and political networks. When they started to echo these fantasies in clinical and non-clinical spaces, they created their own communal networks and told stories about how they had overcome obstacles in the path of a proper medical examination. Without being embedded in these networks, there is no place to tell these stories and get inspired to echo these fantasies in everyday practice.

The second group of doctors highlighted the structural limitations, political dead ends, and other forms of structural violence and
inequality as reasons hindering the implementation of this regulation
properly. They had a cynical attitude vis-à-vis the regulation's capacity
to bring justice. Not engaged with other progressive doctors and often
feeling isolated and alone in their task of documentation, they were
only partially invested in this fantasy. The limits of this fantasy are
more palpable for doctors who were working in the emergency ward
as part of their rotation. They see medical-report preparation only
as a bureaucratic burden to their already busy schedule. There is no
importance they could attribute to forensic documentation as they are
outside the political sociality that can make them affectively invested
in the struggle for proper medical documentation. Their priority is to
ensure the smooth functioning of the emergency ward and provide
medical care to patients in need of emergency care. In this framework, detainees, especially those who do not have any explicit health
problems, are seen as a bureaucratic burden, not as proper patients.

In conclusion, we should return to the initial question of this
chapter: Can state doctors document state violence? These doctors
can be motivated to produce these documents only to the extent that
they are embedded in political networks outside the hospital that
give meaning to their work by maintaining aspirations that forensic evidence prevents torture. While making visible the scars of the
disproportionate use of force by the police, they operate within a
broader legal framework. The more one is invested in political and
non-clinical expert networks committed to torture documentation,
the more likely they are to produce the idea of a unified state through
their commitment to legally sanctioned forensic fantasies and their
belief in state institutions' responsibility and capacity to properly
address human rights violations. This can explain the continuity of
state violence despite a growing pile of (now electronic) documents
attesting to state violence, yet producing no concrete consequences
for the prevention or moderation of violence.

CHAPTER 4

The Necropolitics of
Phantasmal Documents

N o one could have imagined that the question of how to treat ill prisoners would be one of the top agenda items during the negotiations between the Kurdish armed movement and the Turkish state in the aftermath of the war that cost the lives of more than forty thousand people and caused the displacement of more than one million civilians since 1984. At the beginning of the negotiations in 2013, Abdullah Öcalan, the imprisoned leader of PKK, stated that peace cannot take place unless ill prisoners were released.[1] Öcalan was not asking for a special release of imprisoned PKK guerillas but asking state official to implement the existing legal framework and release ill prisoners on moral grounds if their illness was diagnosed at medical-expert institutions. This could not be a topic of bargain, he added; it was the most basic humanitarian situation. The government approached this demand positively and formed a parliamentary commission to listen to the representatives of TUHAD-FED (Federation of Associations for Legal Aid and Solidarity with Families of Arrestees and Convicts, Tutuklu ve Hükümlü Aileleri Hukuk Dayanışma Dernekleri Federasyonu) and PKK convicts about the problems and demands of sick prisoners. Some amendments were made in the legal framework that would expand the scope of the article regulating the conditions under which a sick prisoner can be released. Negotiations failed, and not a single ill prisoner was released. The Kurdish movement has since then made statements to the effect that the state's attitude toward ill prisoners was a litmus test that demonstrated its sincerity about peace. A recent incident concerning the Kurdish politician and former member of the Turkish Parliament Aysel Tuğluk, who got sick in prison, is the ultimate example of how humanitarian regulations about ill prisoners can be easily suspended when it concerns political inmates and how forensic fantasies diffuse into political movements and ideologies through these medical humanitarian regulations.

Aysel Tuğluk was being held in Kocaeli No. 1 Type-F Prison when she was diagnosed with dementia by the doctors in the Departments of Psychiatry, Internal Medicine, Neurology and Forensic Medicine at Kocaeli University Hospital in March 2021. In their report, these doctors wrote that Tuğluk would not be able to stay in prison alone and recommended her release. However, Tuğluk was not released, but instead was referred to the CFM, where she was examined again. The doctors at the Council however concluded that she was medically suitable for serving her sentence. According to the Kurdish movement, the government was using Aysel Tuğluk as a hostage by putting pressure on the doctors at the CFM to prepare reports that would not recognize her illness. Tuğluk's lawyers and human rights activists have circulated the university hospital's medical reports, medical test results, and the testimonies of her cell friends and family members that attest to her rapidly progressive dementia to convince the public that she could not stay in prison. Both the Kurdish political movement and Aysel Tuğluk's representatives seemed to have been drawn to a forensic fantasy, which kept them motivated to search for the "right" medical documents that would put the legal mechanisms into motion by acknowledging her illness and facilitating her release by resorting to Article 16 in Law 5275 that regulates the "postponement of execution due to illness."

Regardless of how detailed, scientific, or convincing these documents are, they failed to convince state officials, especially judges and prosecutors. It seems that state officials were not legally, ethically, or emotionally moved by these documents and their truth-bearing capacity. On the contrary, they came up with new administrative and bureaucratic excuses to render her medical reports irrelevant and prevent her release. Forensic fantasies about the power and efficacy of medical documents in benefiting ill prisoners keep failing.

After months of campaigning, the execution of the ten-year prison sentence against politician Aysel Tuğluk was finally postponed in October 2022. However, almost a year later, the police detained her again at her home based on an investigation dating back to 2012. She was taken to the prosecutor's office and brought before the Duty Heavy Penal Court. The judge asked Tuğluk if she remembered the 2012 rally and her speech. When Tuğluk stated that she did not remember anything, the questioning ended, and she was released again. While she was in custody, Tuğluk's lawyers submitted her medical report to the court. It was as if the courts had forgotten about her medical condition, and her lawyers and family found themselves back at square one, trying to convince the state of her illness over and over again.

How and why did the suffering of ill prisoners come to take central stage during and after the negotiations of a three-decade-long conflict? How did medical documents about sick prisoners become the object of phantasmal investment among radical political actors? The answer to these questions lies in the local histories of prison resistance in Turkey. Especially since the 1980 coup d'état, political prisoners frequently undertook hunger strikes and death fasts as a self-mutilating form of resistance that created a pool of ill bodies in prisons, which in turn facilitated interactions between the human rights movement, progressive doctors, radical political groups, and state officials. It is during these interactions that forensic fantasies were cultivated and gradually captivated the political imagination of radical political movements. The sick, wounded, and dying bodies of prisoners always pose a danger to the biopolitical paradigm of the modern state, for which the reproduction of living subjects in its care is an important source of legitimation. The question of illness and death taking place while a person is under the care of the state reveals the limits of the state control over the lives of its citizens and thus over its sovereignty. Forensic fantasy in the case of ill prisoners in that sense assumes a structural relationship between documentation of illness and welfare of the citizen who is under the state care.

In Turkey, in the last two decades medical documents that embody these forensic fantasies emerged as a site of contention between political groups and state officials. These medical documents testifying prisoners' sickness became the symptom of the state officials' investment in medical rationalities as a governmental strategy. As opposed to most bureaucratic documents that attained their power through invisibility and ordinariness (Brenneis 2006), forensic documents regarding the health condition of prisoners have attained phantasmal character as they were invested with the desires of the opponents of the state. Prisoners, human rights activists, and progressive doctors find themselves increasingly connected to the biopolitical rationalities as the primary reference point of their discourses and practices about prisoners' right to health and the state's responsibilities vis-à-vis its citizens.[2] In previous chapters, I discussed how state-employed doctors or doctors working in the field of human rights are invested in forensic fantasies to varying degrees in their interactions with tortured or dead bodies. Here my focus is the interactions between state officials and dissident groups around the suffering bodies of political prisoners and specifically how forensic documents are produced, circulated, used, or discarded through the fantasies mobilized by state officials, doctors, human rights activists, and insurgent groups. I first tell the story of how bodies of the ill prisoners and medical documents about these prisoners' health status came to occupy a central position in political imagination during the 2000 hunger strike as a critical event that set the groundwork for the fetishization of medical documents. Then I focus on how doctors within and outside the Council witnessed the suffering of hunger strikers, somewhat enabling a long-term trust between progressive doctors and dissident groups. It is through such personal networks that medical humanitarian reasoning expanded among the political groups as well as among human rights activists in the coming years. Without these connections, forensic fantasies would not find roots in and be sustainable among dissident groups. Finally, I discuss how forensic documents politically shape prisoners' life trajectories, thereby turning them into contested political objects. Overall, I demonstrate that the analytics of forensic fantasy is helpful to understand the workings of sovereign practices as well as radical political mobilizations.

Governing the Death Fast with Forensic Documents

In October 2000, political prisoners from three radical political organizations[3] on the Turkish Left declared a hunger strike protest to stop the government's decision to transfer all political prisoners to high-security prisons (Bargu 2014b). Soon after, they made a new statement that said they were going to continue fasting until their death (also known as a death fast, or *ölüm orucu*) unless the high-security prison project was suspended. The representatives of civil-society institutions, intellectuals, and human rights activists mediated negotiations between the representatives of hunger strikers and the government. However, negotiations ended abruptly when the government carried out a military operation called "Return to Life" (*Hayata Dönüş*) on December 19, 2000. Hunger strikers were transferred to hospitals, forcibly fed, and then sent to the newly built high-security prisons. None of these actions ended the hunger strike. On the contrary, political prisoners from other political groups joined the strike in solidarity. The government double downed on its original plan to open the high-security prisons, while confronting the problem of numerous rapidly ailing bodies in prisons as hundreds of hunger strikers moved closer to the brink of death each day.

The health of the first group of hunger strikers began to worsen toward the middle of 2001. The government's response to this full-blown biopolitical crisis was unprecedented. By mobilizing two articles that regulate the compassionate release of prisoners for health reasons, the chief public prosecutor began to release political prisoners. The first is the presidential pardon regulated in Article 104 of the Constitution, which allows the president to intervene "to alleviate penalties or suspend them for a person with chronic illness, disability or for the reason of aging." The second is Article 399 in Law 1412 (Article 16 in Law 5275, i.e. Law on the Execution of Sentences and Security Measures, after 2004) that regulates the "postponement of execution due to illness." According to Article 16, "If the execution of the prison sentence even in this way [i.e., in sections allocated for prisoners in official healthcare institutions] presents an absolute danger for the life of the convict, its execution shall be postponed until he is cured." Before 2004, the article specified no restrictions over the institution that is entitled to deliver a report that attests to prisoners' illnesses. However, during the hunger strike beginning in May 2001, the chief public prosecutor began releasing prisoners only based on reports issued by the CFM that demonstrated the prisoners' lives were at risk.

Even though there were a few cases of seriously ill prisoners released on compassionate grounds throughout the 1980s and 1990s, this recent wave of release was unprecedented because between May 2001 and March 2002, the sentences of 234 convicts were suspended based on the reports prepared by the CFM.[4] Between 2000 and 2001, CFM issued a "cannot stay in prison" report for almost every hunger striker. According to research conducted in the CFM in 2003, 325 out of 344 hunger strikers, who were transferred to the Council to receive medico-legal reports, were diagnosed with Wernicke-Korsakoff syndrome.[5] Some of these prisoners later benefited from presidential pardon as well.[6] By 2004, 109 people died as a result of hunger strikes in prisons, and 614 people were suffering from hunger strike–related illnesses, primarily that of Wernicke-Korsakoff syndrome.[7] Overall, it is estimated that more than 500 prisoners were released for having developed Wernicke-Korsakoff syndrome.[8] All in all, the government did not want to confront or address the political consequences of the deaths of hundreds of people in prisons and preferred to solve the political crisis precipitated by the pending deaths in the mass hunger strike by resorting to technical and medical processes and discharged ill and dying prisoners from prison.[9] This mass release of prisoners was an extraordinary act that fundamentally transformed the role of the CFM as well as forensic medical reports in addressing the problems of ill prisoners. Assuming that prisoners were forced to participate in a hunger strike by their political organizations, the government hoped to divide the movement and end hunger strikes by reprieving prisoners' sentences on medical grounds. This was a covert amnesty legalized with the aid of official medical certificates. However, the government's expectation proved wrong. The hunger strike continued both inside and outside the prison even after these mass discharges.[10]

During these years, three different governments came to power, but the state policy toward hunger strikers was not influenced by these changes in government.[11] Toward the end of 2002, after the general elections, the new AKP government made new appointments at the CFM. By mid-2003, right-wing and conservative media outlets began to raise concerns about the discharge of numerous leftist political prisoners. This is when the Third Specialization Board started to issue forensic reports stating that Wernicke-Korsakoff patients are either fully or partially recovered. In other words, the prisoners who were released because of this syndrome were now considered recovered. This sudden policy change was shocking to families and supporters of hunger strikers as well as to human rights activists because Wernicke-Korsakoff syndrome was identified as a permanent illness in the previous documents issued by the CFM. This change meant that those who were discharged in previous years could be put back in prisons if their reports were not renewed because the illness clause required that the released prisoners must visit the Third Specialization Board of the CFM every six months in order to have the postponement of the execution of their sentence continued. The Human Rights Association organized a press statement on December 27, 2003, in front of the CFM to protest this situation. The association's statement reads as follows: "Since September 2002 we are witnessing a change in government policy, but we have not seen any scientific explanations or articles regarding the miraculous recoveries of Wernicke-Korskakoff patients. . . . We suspect that the CFM is distancing itself from being scientific; it carries out forensic expertise not on the basis of scientific facts, but on political or ideological judgments and prejudices. . . . We have the right to know the reasons behind these negative medical reports."[12]

The representatives of the Human Rights Foundation of Turkey also made public statements regarding the risks of sending these people back to prison: this would interrupt their treatment, including the physical therapy that many of them were receiving at the foundation. They also argued that the mental perception of a Wernicke-Korsakoff patient tends to be limited and they cannot benefit from the corrective aspects of prison at all.[13] However, none of these reversed the situation. On the contrary, the government took another step in 2004 that would further empower the CFM and its documents. That was in the form of an amendment in the compassionate release article according to which the postponement decision of the chief public prosecutor's office should be based "upon a report issued by the Council of Forensic Medicine or issued by the health committee of a fully equipped hospital designated by the Ministry of Justice and approved by the Council of Forensic Medicine." This regulation perpetuated the power of the official expert authority on issues concerning forensic medicine and forensic sciences, including the investigation and documentation of prisoner illnesses. In other words, the legally valid forensic knowledge production about ill prisoners was centralized in the hands of this Council. Its forensic documents were considered more truthful by the law while rendering all other reports less relevant and effective.

In response to this policy change, some hunger strikers filed complaints against the CFM doctors with the help of the Turkish Medical Association, accusing the former of issuing contradictory medical reports. Lawyers of some patients even appealed to the European Court of Human Rights (ECHR) on the grounds that their clients could not care for themselves in prison and the CFM reports were partial. The ECHR decided that an independent medical team consisting of two French doctors and one Turkish doctor should examine the Wernicke-Korsakoff patients who were imprisoned or were going to be imprisoned again.[14] In a sense, the Turkish state and the ECHR alike trapped the political prisoners within the nets of medical diagnoses. Medical reports emerged again as the only legitimate ground for discussing the consequences of hunger strikes. Those who refused to be examined by this international team of doctors were withheld from all legal, bureaucratic, and medical frameworks. They became fugitives. They either fled the country to live in one of the European countries as illegal immigrants or suffered from the troubles of a fugitive life within the country. The only way for prisoners to be recognized by law was to allow local and foreign physicians and psychiatrists to read illness symptoms on their bodies and in their minds.[15] The increasingly arbitrary process of medicalization of the hunger strike through forensic documents rendered the protesters extremely vulnerable vis-à-vis the state. While some hunger strikers were released, others were taken back to prison. Not knowing what the CFM's diagnosis would be—namely, whether they would get a positive or negative report—an atmosphere of panic and suspense began to surround the strikers and their families. Nothing was foreseeable. The state rendered itself unreadable via forensic reports issued by its CFM.

With the extensive use of the illness clause and forensic reports to solve the hunger strike crisis, politics of hunger strikes has increasingly boiled down to the questions of medical intervention, diagnosis, and evidence. As Veena Das noted in another case, even "those who were locked in a combative relationship with the state" were "pulled into the gravitational force of the state through the circulation of documents produced by its functionaries" (Das 2004, 229). Many hunger strikers ended up visiting independent medical nongovernmental organizations to have their illnesses documented to make a case for the extension of the reprieve of their sentence at the court. As the state established itself as an entity beyond and above the people through the illegibility of its medical documents, political prisoners were increasingly bound up with the fantasies of medical documents for these documents became the main determinants of their life trajectories.

Bureaucratic papers and documents tend to operate as invisible mediators of state bureaucracies. So in order to restore the visibility of documents, Hull (2012) invites us to "look at rather than through them." Medical documents issued by hospitals or the CFM about ill prisoners increased their visibility and importance throughout the 2010s. Rather than being routine bureaucratic documents, these documents increasingly gained a phantasmal quality to the extent that they are seen as emblematic of governmental workings of the state and become constitutive of alternative publics and coalitions concerning ill prisoners. Some doctors who are sympathetic with the suffering of hunger strikers and work both within and outside the CFM were important in the formation of alternative forensic communities and knowledges.

Doctors' Testimony to Prisoners' Suffering and the Production of Forensic Fantasies for Political Activists

Doctors who are working in the field of human rights emerged as important actors during the hunger strike that took place between 2000 and 2006. Some of them were the firsthand witnesses of these events from within the CFM, and some others were working in the Turkish Medical Association, the Human Rights Foundation of Turkey, or the Foundation for Society and Legal Studies (Toplum ve Hukuk Araştırmaları Vakfı, TOHAV). These doctors met the hunger strikers in prisons or after their release and provided medical treatment, followed their health conditions, or produced medical documents regarding the prognosis of their illness.

When the death fast started to affect the health of hundreds of prisoners, doctors from the Turkish Medical Association formed teams to regularly visit and examine the hunger strikers after securing permission from the Ministry of Justice. The Human Rights Foundation of Turkey and TOHAV were the two other human rights organizations that specialize in providing rehabilitation treatment for the hunger strikers who got Wernicke-Korsakoff either because of forced feeding or long-term hunger. Dr. Umutcan, who is a human right activist who worked as a volunteer at the Human Rights Foundation of Turkey at the time, remembers how she and other doctors could not cope up with the sheer number of applicants in the initial months of release of hunger strikers. The Human Rights Foundation of Turkey invited all doctors who volunteered to help hunger strikers when, in her words, "Hundreds of prisoners who were no different from a bag of bones were released. The state did not even provide them with ambulances to take them to their homes. We as human rights activists took them from prisons. The Human Rights Foundation of Turkey and TOHAV treated them." The treatment of some hunger strikers still continues in these non-governmental organizations.

Dr. Kaya was one of the doctors that visited the hunger strikers in prison in one of the medical support teams formed by the Turkish Medical Association. When I first met Dr. Kaya, she was working as a full-time doctor at the Human Rights Foundation of Turkey and vividly remembered those days. She witnessed how most of the hunger strikers contracted Wernicke-Korsakoff syndrome because of force-feeding at the hospitals, turning them into two-and-a-half-year-old babies whey they woke up. She knew from earlier hunger strike experiences in Turkey that injecting glucose directly into a blood vessel without mixing it with B1 vitamins caused irreversible brain damage known as Wernicke-Korsakoff syndrome. However, despite doctors' warnings, many hunger strikers were subjected to wrong medical treatment after they were brought to hospitals when they lost consciousness and when their families allowed the doctors to force-feed them. According to Dr. Kaya, "This was done intentionally to disable these people. Their deaths could have been prevented but they were sent to death. When they re-gained their consciousness, they tore the serum off. There was a constant struggle between their will and bodily endurance. Forced feeding turned into a kind of torture for them." It is doctors' witnessing of wrong medical

practices that motivated many of them to continue to provide treatment for hunger strikers when they were released. For many doctors
who work in these organizations, the state released hunger strikers
in order not to take responsibility for their treatment. The Human
Rights Foundation of Turkey and the Turkish Medical Association
prepared reports that drew upon the latest scientific work on the
bodily consequences of long-term hunger and concluded that it is
extremely rare that Wernicke-Korsakoff patients recover; the reports
highlighted the inconsistency of the CFM's medical documents.

For doctors who were sensitive to human rights issues but working in official medical settings such as the CFM, the process was more
traumatic as they had to witness the violence hunger strikers were
subjected to in such settings. Dr. Selen was an intern at the CFM in
2001 and working as a reporter in the Third Specialization Board
when the first group of hunger strikers were brought to the Council
for examination and documentation purposes. The board was com-
posed of twelve doctors from different specialties and convened to
decide whether these prisoners could take care of themselves in the
prison. The board members assess patients' previous health records
and ask questions about their current health situation. Dr. Selen has
a vivid memory of how hunger strikers were treated during board
examinations: "It still hurts so much in my heart, and I feel like I'm
losing my nerve when I think of how they were treated during these
examinations. The doctors would push them around in the chair they
sat in and say things like 'stand up,' 'walk,' 'do this,' 'do that.' They were
just too weak. They could not walk, stand up, or even move. Most of
them had either just quit the hunger strike or had been on it for over
200 days, feeling overtired. The doctors would not let anyone else
accompany the patients. Inglorious men! I still feel traumatized by
the death fast."

Forensic doctors like Dr. Selen were appalled by the attitude of
some doctors in the Council and wanted to approach hunger strikers as patients and refused to see them as terrorists, criminals, or
political prisoners. After seeing the reports that showed these prisoners had recovered, Dr. Selen decided to carry out research on the

forensic analysis of hunger strikers, focusing on the prognosis of long-term starvation to determine if one can ever recover from this syndrome. Even though she faced some resistance from within the Council, she was able to finish the research.[16] She says: "I wanted to make the argument that this illness, Wernicke-Korsakoff, does not lessen over time, that one does not recover from it. The government was releasing prisoners very quickly at first. But in six months or so they somehow changed their minds and started to put some of the hunger strikers back in prison. The way they did this was like this; they said: 'Look, the patients that you said cannot recover are dancing the *halay*, going to weddings, protests, etc.' But we are not saying that these people cannot use their bodies, we are saying that their brain is damaged."

She said she only later realized why some professors did not want her to do this research. Because the government was planning to imprison the hunger strikers again. The research demonstrated some gaps in the scientific reports prepared by CFM and insufficiencies of medical examinations of hunger strikers. Doctors like Dr. Selen found themselves in a conflictual position vis-à-vis the Council, and they were pushed toward its margins. Some of them were not promoted or were forced to quit. Some of these doctors collaborated with the doctors who work in the field of human rights for the rehabilitation of hunger strikers once they quit or retired from their jobs. Dr. Selen was relegated to a post in a small city in Anatolia but did not go; instead she quit her job at the Council.

Another doctor that witnessed the process from within the Council was Dr. Mehmet. After working as an emergency doctor for years, he became an intern at the CFM in 2001, the first year of the hunger strike. At the time of the interview, he was retired from the Council and working as a volunteer at the office of Istanbul Medical Chamber, where we met for the interview. He was one of the progressive doctors who was never promoted at the Council for being an outspoken person about political issues. To him, the ways in which forensic medicine reports were used during the hunger strikes shows how medicine and the CFM are used by political authorities: "The state thought that the hunger strike in prisons will end with the military operation [i.e., *Hayata Dönüş*], but it did not. Then, they came up with another solution: covert amnesty. They did it via the CFM. They gave Wernicke-Korsakoff reports to end the strike resistance, yet this also did not work." He was very critical of the policy change at the time because this meant that "either the first wave of certificates prepared by the Council were false, or the recent ones were. Both options created serious suspicion regarding those scientists who prepared the certificates. This was a grave violation of medical ethics." For him, the fact that the government used certificates to release prisoners and then put them back in prison shows the instrumentalization of medicine and the government's control over medical-certificate-production processes.

Before he started his position at the CFM, Dr. Mehmet was a member of the Turkish Medical Association, which was then providing active medical support for the hunger strikers by organizing prison visits with voluntary doctors. The Turkish Medical Association had permission from the Ministry of Justice to organize these visits to observe the health of prisoners and provide medical knowledge. Having the memory of the previous hunger strike in 1996, in which the prisoners were force-fed without their consent in state hospitals, the prisoners were suspicious of doctors in general. In order to gain their trust, the Turkish Medical Association's doctors told the patients that they respected their protest and were not there to force-feed them. They were only going to check on them so that the hunger strikers could continue their protest without potentially damaging their bodies or brains. The doctors wanted to make sure that the hunger strikers took vitamin B1 alongside water, salt, and sugar so that their brains remained unharmed.[17] The fact that hunger strikers were taking vitamin B1 allowed them to survive more than three hundred days without losing consciousness. Doctors were also informing them of their rights as patients and asking at what stage of the strike they would give consent to medical intervention, if at all.[18] He explained: "When we first got to the prison, they did not trust us. It took time to convince them that we understood and respected their decision to go on hunger strike, and that we were against force-feeding, and we were there just to check on them regularly and to make life easier for them during their protest as well as to try to take measures so that they will not be physically or mentally damaged at the end of their protests."

Informed consent documents from the Turkish Medical Association emphasize that medical examinations, check-ups, and follow-ups should not be considered interventions in a hunger strike. This notice is printed under each informed consent document prepared for prisoners: "These medical practices do not aim to feed you, but only to provide you with medical support." Over time the Turkish Medical Association doctors and hunger strikers built a relationship of trust. Dr. Mehmet notes how he used to feel during these visits: "We did our best not to show them the deep contradiction we experienced then. We respected the decision they made but we also saw the inevitable consequences of the death fast." There were ten prisoners from two different death-fast groups (people were joining the strike neither individually nor en masse but by forming groups) in the prison he regularly visited. All of them had already lost a quarter of their body weight, some of them more. They were under serious medical risk. They suffered from muscle pain, diarrhea, extreme sensitivity to light, nausea, and sleep disruption. When they stood up, they felt dizzy and lost their balance. During these regular visits, Dr. Mehmet became friends with many hunger strikers. In 2001, when he began to work at the Third Specialization Board at the CFM, he saw some of the prisoners he became friends with when he was part of the Turkish Medical Association team. These were extremely dramatic encounters for him: "I will especially never forget the visit of two prisoners whom I knew earlier. One of them was Meliha. We used to chat a lot in prison when I went to check on them. I saw her at the CFM. She didn't recognize me. Her sight was blurred. The other was Lale. During one of our prison visits they had sung us songs and marches. I saw her at the CFM too. She was suffering from pellagra caused by vitamin B deficiency. The CFM issued a report stating that she cannot stay in prison."

Being firsthand witnesses to the suffering of the hunger strikers, doctors like Mehmet and Selen mobilized their expert knowledge for human rights purposes both within and outside the CFM. Progressive doctors wanted to help the rehabilitation and treatment of hunger strikers and documentation of their illness as the firsthand medical witnesses of their suffering. It is their commitment to ethical principles in their interaction with hunger strikers and their respectful attitude toward hunger strikers that paved the way for the development of long-term trust between these doctors and hunger strikers. There emerged an intimate and informal network of solidarity between doctors and political activists that would keep forensic fantasies alive for political activists.

The mass release of hunger strikers with the CFM reports and the emergent connections between doctors and political activists foregrounded forensic knowledge and reporting in discussions of prisoners' health-related suffering in general. Toward the end of the 2010s, prisoners suffering from different kinds of illnesses also began to appeal for postponement of their sentences through the compassionate release article. In less than a decade, the topic of ill prisoners and the problems of documentation of illness at the CFM was on the agenda of human rights groups, political parties, and the Kurdish political movement, which would regularly turn to doctors as medical experts that would validate prisoners' rights to health care through documents they provide.

When Do Phantasmal Documents Work?

The illness clause was not frequently discussed in the public sphere before 2000. Research into newspaper archives and parliamentary debates yield very limited results, suggesting that the visibility of ill prisoners before 2000 was quite restricted. Even though Article 399, which regulated the suspension of execution of a penalty in the case of a serious illness was in effect since the early twentieth century, it had rarely been invoked.[19] The question of ill prisoners was not on the

agenda of the Turkish Left or Kurdish parties and human rights organizations as a systematic problem that warranted political or medical
attention.

The first public campaign concerning ill prisoners sought the
discharge of Güler Zere. Although Zere had been convicted of being
a member of an illegal Marxist organization, the campaign demanding her release was publicized with humanitarian and human rights
slogans. It is no coincidence that the Zere campaign was initiated
by those affiliated with one of the three radical organizations on the
Turkish Left that started the death fast in 2000 and thus were familiar with the legal process concerning the release of ill prisoners.

Zere fell ill with cancer in the Elbistan Prison in the southeastern
province of Kahramanmaraş in the last months of 2008, after having
served fourteen years of her sentence. When her condition worsened
after the operation she had in early 2009, she was transferred to the
prisoner ward of Çukurova University Hospital, where doctors prepared a medical report that states that Zere is a heavily disabled person whose life is under serious risk and needs care and supervision
by another person as well as intense and severe treatment including
radiotherapy, which cannot be provided under prison conditions.
Therefore, it is advisable to postpone her sentence until she recov-
ers.[20] Despite this university hospital report, the public prosecutor
was required by law to demand the certification of this report by
the CFM. The Third Specialization Board, which is responsible from
preparing reports concerning the suspension of the execution of
penalty,[21] could have just certified the report without seeing Zere in
person since it was a medical emergency, but the board insisted on
examining her, thus delaying a final decision in her case.[22]

Public prosecutors avoid using medical reports prepared by
university hospitals, which they regard as less "official" than medical reports prepared by the CFM, because the former needs to be
eventually certified by the CFM according to Article 16. As a result,
prosecutors often order ill prisoners across Turkey to be transferred
to Istanbul's CFM headquarters in unventilated, dirty, and window-
less prisoner transport vehicles to receive official expert reports. The

ill prisoners refer to this transfer process as "report torture" (*Rapor işkencesi*). This torturous transfer process is presented by state officials as the only way for the bureaucratic process to move forward. Yet, only a small percent of ill prisoners receives positive reports from the CFM that would grant them postponement of their sentence.[23] Most prisoners simply end up exhausted by the trip, which dashes their hopes for discharge and blocks their access to proper medical care outside the prison. Subsequently, their lawyers may file an appeal against the reports issued by the CFM, starting the bureaucratic process all over again.

Zere was transferred to Istanbul via a fourteen-hour trip on July 6, 2009. However, the final CFM report did not certify the conclusion in the report issued by the university hospital. It concluded instead with a contrary assessment: "Her treatment can continue in the prisoner ward of the Çukurova Hospital."[24] Zere's lawyers objected to this report, pointing out the contradiction between the two expert reports. The CFM agreed to discuss this contradiction at its general assembly's next meeting. However, Zere's case could not be discussed for months due to the fact that there were some medical reports missing in her file. Zere spent this time waiting in a prisoner ward in an Istanbul hospital. These ad hoc rooms that are converted into prisoner wards are located in the basement of hospitals and are often dark, dirty, and unhygienic spaces. Guards often used handcuffs to tie Zere to her hospital bed during her treatment. Two soldiers continuously watched over her. Because contact with families and attendants are kept at a minimum, she was not allowed to have a family attendant stay with her in the hospital room.

Toward the end of the summer of 2009, many state officials from the Ministry of Justice to the president's office began to face questions about the fate of Güler Zere. The circulation of a picture of Zere lying in the fetal position on a bed in the prison ward, with a policeman standing next to her, contributed to the publicity of her case. Human rights activists and different political groups organized campaigns, marches, and press statements demanding "Freedom for Güler Zere." Even the columnists of right-wing newspapers wrote articles supporting the discharge of Zere and her right to access medical care. Political groups and organizations affiliated with the People's Front (Halk Cephesi), of which Güler Zere was a member, were drawn toward the CFM and organized a month-long sit-in in front of it in August 2009 in order to protest the delays in the Council's reporting process.

The CFM needed further documents from the hospital regarding Zere's latest condition to prepare its final assessment. Her lawyers were trying to submit medical reports stamped with a date that preceded the meeting by only a few days in order not to compromise the validity of the reports. If the reports were considered not to be up to date, the Council could have postponed the meeting. Given the fact that Zere's health condition was continuously deteriorating, her latest medical assessment deemed her condition unstable. It took a lot of time and energy on the part of her lawyers and family to make sure that they had her latest medical reports ready right before the general meeting of the Council. Her father describes their experiences concerning these reports as follows:

> We've sent a pack of reports. We are embarrassed to ask for further reports from doctors here [Çukurova University Hospital]. They [CFM] keep saying that "a file is missing." The process got stuck at the Council of Forensic Medicine. They do not want to discharge her, they want to kill her. This is the truth behind it. Our lawyers are trying hard, we are working hard. Most recently, they asked for another medical report. We sent it. She just had another operation, so we had to send a new report. Then they found some missing documents in her file again. Then a friend of us sent it to them, but all this to no avail.[25]

On November 4, 2009, approximately four months after Zere's first examination at the CFM, the Third Specialization Board finally gathered to prepare its ultimate report. The report testified that her illness was permanent and that there was no prospect of recovery, recommending that she should be released. The then President Abdullah Gül intervened and pardoned Güler Zere amid the public outcry for her release.[26] After her release, Zere said: "When I was released from prison, it was too late. They brought me next to death and left me there. My right to life was usurped. I was given the right to die outside the prison. I will never forget this."[27] She passed away only seven months later.[28]

Like Zere, most prisoners are discharged only when their illness reaches a terminal stage. As the ill prisoners are transferred between institutions, waiting for the necessary documents to be prepared, verified, and circulated among institutions, they are reduced to the "status of living dead" in prison wards of hospitals or prisons. As human rights lawyer Sevgul, who deals with numerous cases of ill prisoners as part of the Human Rights Association, says, "They are delivered to their families half-dead."[29] The events surrounding Zere's illness and campaign for her release demonstrate the central role that medical documents played in the service of the necropolitical practices of the state, and, concurrently, how they contributed to prisoners' struggles for their rights. The slowness of the document-preparation processes was at the center of the activist campaign demanding her release.

The central role of the forensic documents in making decisions about the prisoners' right to life and access to health is shaped not only by the legal framework and its gaps but also through the struggles of the families, human rights activists, and doctors who have been keeping the suffering of ill prisoners on the public agenda. These struggles are informed by forensic fantasies as well as the knowledge that the state is not an overarching unified entity. Despite the fact that the AKP government's policy has been to keep ill prisoners in prison as long as possible regardless of the level of their illness, there are gaps and inconsistencies in the bureaucratic mechanisms that put these documents into practice. The Güler Zere campaign was an example of this. This campaign was the precursor of other forms of protests for the rights of ill prisoners. The government's response against the popularization of the cause of ill prisoners was to increase its discretionary power in issues concerning ill prisoners via changes in the legal framework.

The criterion of the "absolute danger to life" in Article 16 turns into an absolute expectation of death because legal authorities are reluctant to discharge any political prisoner who can even partially recover from their illness after such a discharge. The CFM doctors write their reports according to this unstable criterion and declare their opinions at the end of their reports as to whether the prisoner is fit to live in prison on their own. Most of the prisoners who receive reports affirming their terminal condition are often in the final stages of their illness. In many cases, the moment when they received the decision of postponement, they are either effectively unconscious or extremely ill, conditions that necessitate their immediate transfer to intensive care units for better treatment. Many of them survive only for a couple of months after their discharge. If not, they die before their discharge decision.[30] The ill prisoners and the documents concerning their rights, health status, and medical treatment are continuously bounced between the prison, the courthouse, the hospital, and the CFM. This mundane state practice of circulating prisoners and official documents across different agencies reveals the extent to which a bureaucracy operates in relation to ill prisoners, inflicting necropolitical violence via forensic documents that often contributes to the premature death of ill prisoners. This is what I call the "necropolitical violence of phantasmal documents."

When Do Phantasmal Documents Not Work? The Case of Politically Dangerous Ill Prisoners

The Güler Zere campaign increased political and social awareness about the plight of ill prisoners. Human rights activists and political groups realized that they could make a collective case for the rights of ill prisoners by making them visible. Two key events ensued in the following years. In 2010, only a year after Zere's release, the Istanbul branch of the Human Rights Association started a regular sit-in

protest for the rights of ill prisoners. These vigils are called F-Type
sit ins in protest of the F-Type high-security prison system, and the
association's main demand is the release of ill prisoners. The other
key event, the release of ill political prisoners, was on the list of the
Kurdish political movement during the peace negotiation.

Prisoners' rights movements have been informed by forensic
fantasies and have been keeping biologically based rights' claims at
its center. Given the high number of political prisoners in Turkish
prisons, many ill political prisoners have familial, social, or political
networks that provide support, guidance, and solidarity. Ordinary
prisoners who are seriously ill would also be taken up and publicized
by political groups or human rights groups. Human rights activists,
relatives of political prisoners, and radical political groups sought
to create alternative public spaces to reach a wider audience and to
make the suffering of ill prisoners visible.[31] For this, they also relied
on reports obtained from university hospitals and the CFM, and
they made biopolitical claims in favor of ill prisoners. These practices
aimed to rescue forensic documents from being solely an instrument
of necropolitical violence so that they are given new visibility and
effectiveness in these alternative public spaces. For example, during
the F-Type vigils, people from the Prison Commission of the Human
Rights Association (İnsan Hakları Derneği Hapishane Komisyonu)
sit in the form of a capital F—a letter that symbolizes F-Type high-
security prisons—while holding up medical reports documenting
the illnesses of prisoners. There are two banners in these protests,
which read: "The isolation policy kills. Close down F-type prisons!"
and "We do not want any more deaths in prison. Discharge seriously
ill prisoners!" Protest participants stand behind these banners and
hold them aloft. They also carry the pictures of ill prisoners and A3-
size posters with the names of ill prisoners and their illnesses, such
as the following: "Özgür Uygun: paralyzed," "Siraç Toğluk: severe
cardiac patient," "Fesih Aslan: 80% mental retardation," "Fatih Gül:
advanced tuberculosis," "Fırat Özçelik: brain overgrowth." This is
an uncanny form of protest where the onlooker is invited to witness the slow death of ill prisoners through photographs of them

alongside these forensic description of their illness. The medical diagnoses of the prisoners' illnesses are turned into slogans to make demands for the suspension of the execution of a penalty. Protestors read these forensic documents about ill prisoners prepared by general hospitals, university hospitals, or the CFM alongside the letters from ill prisoners to put pressure on relevant political and bureaucratic authorities by making their suffering visible. The prisoners' letters often describe the progression of the illness, the kind of medical treatment the ill prisoner has received or was denied, how the prisoner currently feels, who takes care of the prisoner behind bars, or what kind of diet is needed. If the relatives or lawyers of the prisoner are at the protest, they also narrate the most recent information available on the prisoner's health and the bureaucratic obstacles they have encountered in order to see a doctor, access medical treatment, or obtain medico-legal reports from the CFM. Drawing upon the principles of medical ethics and national and international conventions, they challenge the legal practices that reproduce the marginality of political prisoners by substantiating forensic reports with prisoners' personal illness stories. At a broader level, this is a very effective way of mobilizing humanitarian sentiments and forensic fantasies among the wider population, considering the government's insistence on classifying ill political prisoners as a "dangerous population." Resorting to the state's claim of biopolitical protection becomes effective only if the prisoner is classified as a human being whose life is valuable.

The initial version of the regulation stated that ill prisoners could resort to this article only if the execution of their sentence presented "an absolute danger to the life of the convict." The government made an amendment to the regulation in 2013 during the negotiations with the Kurdish armed movement and added that those who could not take care of themselves in prison can also request a reprieve of the execution of their sentence. This enabled a more flexible interpretation of the article. The doctors in the Council and hospitals were thus asked to examine patients and their medical records to answer whether the ill prisoners meet these criteria. However, at the

same time, the government made another amendment that priori-
tized security concerns of the state, according to which even if the
medico-legal report concludes that the ill prisoner should not stay in
prison, the deferral of the sentence is made conditional upon a further assessment by security forces, who must declare that the prisoner 'constitutes no danger in terms of social security.

These struggles and complaints against the arbitrary implementation of the illness article have prompted the government to respond
by amending the article a third time, almost a year and a half after
it had already been revised. The adjectives of "severe or substantial"
(ağır ve somut) were added in front of the clause "danger in terms of
social security" to curtail, at least partially, the arbitrariness of the
clause. According to the new version, "A convict who, due to a severe
illness or disability, cannot sustain life on their own in prison conditions and is not considered to pose a serious and concrete threat
to public safety may have their sentence postponed until recovery
according to the procedure specified in the third paragraph." (Turkish Criminal Law Article 5275 Addendum: 24/1/2013-6411/3)."

One high-profile case in which the contradictions of this clause
became palpable was that of Ramazan Özalp, a Kurdish political prisoner sentenced to twenty years in prison in 1994. Özalp is paralyzed
due to a brain tumor. Medical reports from both the hospital and the
CFM advised postponing his sentence. The prosecutor requested the
written opinion of the anti-terrorism unit and law enforcement officials in his village to ascertain whether Özalp would pose a security
threat to society. After evaluating the opinion of the gendarmerie
along with the forensic medicine report, the prosecutor denied the
release request with the following statement: "He himself does not
pose a threat to the security of society, but in the case of his arrival
at the village of Dirsekli in Idil province, he might be used as a pro-
paganda tool by some political people and citizens, and this might
give rise to various political actions and cause tension and conflict
between citizens with different political views and security forces,
and this situation might be reflected in the press and cause unrest."[32]
In order to protect the social body, he was thereby expended. He was

kept in prison for another eight months before his condition worsened and he was transferred to a hospital. Then he was discharged,
only to live another four months in a private clinic in his hometown.
This "danger to social security" amendment has thus expanded the
discretionary powers of security forces, as well as of political and
legal authorities for whom the bodies and lives of political prisoners
are dangerous to the social body.

This biopolitical contradiction between the protection of the
individual body and the social body is resolved through a necropolitical logic that gives authority to the security forces and the ministry of internal affairs. With the legalization of arbitrariness in the
illness clause, medical expertise and documentation concerning ill
prisoners have diminished in importance. The state apparatuses'
conflicting biopolitical priorities vis-à-vis ill political prisoners creates a necropolitical hierarchy between different types of documents.
Which type of document is more likely to contribute to the making
of death for the ill prisoner depends on the political conjuncture, the
current version of the law, and the power struggles between diverse
political groups and state institutions. In other words, a document
might well become both an instrument of necropolitics and one of
biopolitics at different times, depending on the context in which it
is used. Most of the time, a report confirming illness is not suffi-
cient in and of itself to guarantee the discharge of the prisoner. This
report must also be issued, verified, and transferred to the related
authorities on time. Moreover, a report issued by a university hospital might be overruled by a report prepared by the CFM. The CFM
report might be overruled by a document prepared by the police to
keep the ill prisoner behind bars, unless the prisoner's lawyers and
advocates push to start the legal process all over again. Finally, while
medico-legal documents frequently emerge as the death-making
mechanism for some prisoners, these same documents can later be
appropriated by human rights activists to make biopolitical claims
for others in the public space or during court trials. Medical documents are mobile and context-bound entities, and their meaning and
importance change as they circulate. The necropolitical hierarchy of

documents is thus always in the making and reflects the social and political contentions among diverse actors, who are interpellated by forensic fantasies to different degrees and in different ways.

Documents as Necropolitical Fantasies

The Law on the Execution of Sentences and Security Measures is ostensibly designed to provide health care to ill prisoners in line with international conventions. However, the more we scrutinize the daily workings of the relevant article (16), namely the postponement of a sentence due to illness, the more we observe the proliferation of death rather than life, of illness rather than health. The biopolitical protections afforded to prisoners that should work to ensure their health easily slip into necropolitical violence that hastens their death or disability. Necropolitical violence or the making of death in the case of ill prisoners requires more than "letting [the prisoner] die" or "disallowing life to the point of death" in the Foucauldian sense. It requires the involvement of multiple legal and administrative institutions that manage the bureaucratic process by controlling the circulation of documents and, by extension, the fate of ill prisoners. Human rights activists and political parties can also recirculate documents to make biopolitical claims in favor of ill prisoners. Their endurance as material artifacts gives documents unexpected powers as potential evidence of ill treatment and torture, especially when they are put to an alternative use in challenging the state's necropolitical violence. However, availability of medical documents never guarantees one's release. The hope and the belief that these documents might work at some point for some people keep people attached to forensic fantasies. It is an example of "the oscillation between the rational and the magical to become the defining feature of the state in such margins" (Das 2007, 169). However, here the vulnerable and expandable body of the political prisoner becomes the margin of the state where forensic fantasies are doomed to fail.

The F-Type protests or the campaign for the release of Aysel Tuğluk that I opened this chapter with demonstrate how human rights activists and families challenge the necropolitical power of documents and insist on the humanity of the ill prisoners labeled as terrorists, criminals, or enemies of the state. Such protests and over-investment in forensic fantasies draw attention away from the acts committed by these prisoners that landed them in prison in the first place and instead track the progression of their illnesses and the difficulties they endure in securing access to proper medical care. As the critical literature on biological citizenship has shown, there are limits to the use of biology as the basis for demanding political or social citizenship rights. More specifically, the emphasis on bodily suffering might obstruct a person's political agency or the broader political-economic dynamics that cause illness in the first place (Petryna 2002; Ticktin 2011). This framework, however, cannot fully account for the complex repercussions of advocating for ill political prisoners by using their bodily suffering and making biopolitical demands. Given that state officials including prison administrators, guardians, security forces, and even some doctors tend to see the body of the political prisoner primarily as a political entity that poses a danger to the social body, one can argue that there is a resistance on their part to focus solely on the bodily suffering of the ill political prisoner. Forensic fantasies tend to fail when it concerns the bodies of political prisoners because many state officials would never be completely captivated by forensic fantasies and their biological reductionism when it comes to political bodies.

CHAPTER 5

Forensic Fantasies in the Streets

The Turkish government's plans to demolish a major public park in Taksim Square in Istanbul in May 2013 sparked a national wave of protests, which soon turned into what is called the Gezi uprising. Continuing for weeks across the nation, the uprising constituted a people's movement that expressed demands for more democracy and freedom. Protestors voiced diverse grievances against increasing authoritarianism, limits to women's legal rights, environmental concerns, and labor-related issues (Alessandrini, Üstündağ, and Yıldız 2013; Yörük and Yüksel 2014). In response to the protests, police excessively sprayed tear gas on hundreds of thousands of demonstrators—often at close range and in close spaces (Physicians for Human Rights 2013), bringing the question of police violence to the public agenda. The police intervention during the Gezi uprising was violent. Eight young people lost their lives, while fifteen citizens lost their sight. More than eight thousand injuries occurred due to tear gas, rubber bullets, water cannons, beatings, and live ammunition.[1] To draw the public attention away from these unsettling facts, government members strategically trivialized violence and sought to mobilize ambiguities and societal prejudices against the protestors.

The impact of police violence on protestors were different during and after the Gezi uprising due to the massive and relatively long-term character of the protests. Besides the usual political suspects such as the members of Kurdish political organization, radical

Marxist political parties, and feminist organizations, now many young citizens who did not have previous political experience also flooded the streets and became the target of state violence for the first time. This type of collective uprising and the sense of being the collective target of police violence was a unique experience not only for many of the protestors but also doctors who were fighting for human rights.

Like many other professionals, doctors took to the streets of Taksim on the first day of the protests.[2] Initially, doctors were in Gezi Park as protestors. Yet, as police attacks against the protestors became harsher, doctors and medical students found themselves being called upon through their medical-expert identity. Soon after, they started to follow the protestors in order to treat them. Their medical-ethical priorities prevented them from fully engaging in political debates and decision-making processes during the protests, even if they would have liked to. They opted to prioritize the act of caring, mobilizing their professional networks, redoubling their efforts to provide medical treatment, and organizing more temporary infirmaries and first aid units for injured protestors. On the third day of the mass protests approximately fifteen to twenty doctors walked across the crowd in Taksim Square wearing white coats, helmets, goggles, and gasmasks, indicating that they had just been in the middle of clashes helping the protestors. One person from among the protestors shouted, "Doctors are coming!" and hundreds of people stopped, opened the way for them, and clapped their hands as they walked by, and they clapped them back. This expression of solidarity characterized the relationship between the doctors and the protestors throughout the Gezi protests. This was one of the rare moments where doctors and protestors as potential victims of human rights violations stood side by side against the police in a public space. However, their public visibility as coat-wearing doctors was short-lived as they themselves also became the target of police violence.

Turkey is not the only country where health care has been targeted or the idea of medical neutrality is challenged and disputed in times of conflict. For example, Bahraini security forces targeted, abducted, and detained physicians (Physicians for Human Rights 2011, 18) during the riots in 2011. In Egypt in 2011, there was deliberate aggression against doctors and field hospitals in Tahrir Square (Hamdy and Bayoumi 2016). Medical personnel in Ukraine were also attacked by police during clashes between anti-government protestors and riot police in 2014 (Holt 2014).[3] However, the strong tradition of torture documentation in Turkey and doctors' firsthand-witnessing experiences have distinctly informed how these medical experts deal with police violence. As I have discussed in previous chapters, doctors since the 1980s have created connections with the victims of political violence through the human rights organizations. Moreover, they have learned to disguise their political affiliations in order to create a safe and legitimate space for the victims of violence through their medical-witnessing practice in the offices of the Turkish Medical Association[4] and the Human Rights Foundation of Turkey. In a similar vein, during the Gezi uprising, many doctors who were sympathetic toward the protestors wanted to help the victims of police violence and founded or worked at temporary clinics to provide emergency treatment for the injured protestors. Doctors at the Human Rights Foundation of Turkey welcomed both the injured protestors to the foundation and trained the younger generation of doctors to use their medical expertise to treat the injured (in this case, especially injuries due to tear gas, pepper gas, and plastic bullets) and document the consequences of riot-control agents on the bodies of the protestors. Young doctors and medical students volunteered at the association, in makeshift infirmaries, and at the Human Rights Foundation of Turkey.

The profile of most Gezi protestors subjected to police violence was different in the sense that many of the protestors did not have any affiliation with political parties and did not resist the government out of some ideological conviction. Rather they were feeling part of an anonymous group who spontaneously came together to collectively protest the government's demolishment plans about the park while criticizing anti-democratic practices of the government. Despite the pain and suffering they experienced, there was also a strong sense of

accomplishment and collective exhilaration among all Gezi participants including doctors. The question for me is to understand forensic fantasies that inform doctors' torture-documentation practices
during the Gezi uprising. What happens to doctors' forensic fantasies when injured protestors felt that they were making the country
a better place and had the support of the majority of people in the
country without necessarily thinking about the prospective political,
bodily, or emotional price they might be forced to pay. Finally, I want
to understand how doctors in the field of human rights navigated
the tension between their desire to make violence visible and their
emotional engagement with and excitement about the Gezi protests.

The government's hostile policies toward doctors kept them tied
to the medical field as a way of legitimizing their presence through
the discourse of medical ethics and impartiality. The criminalization
of doctors consolidated forensic fantasies while increasing doctors'
distance from the protestors as the forensic and medical gaze often
fails to recognize how collective action and imagination might in
fact heal physical and psychological wounds. Encounters with the
victims of violence during the Gezi protests created an opportunity
for doctors to critically reflect on their own treatment and documentation practices by showing how collective exhilaration helps
people deal with the consequences of state violence. In the following
pages, I first discuss how doctors hold on to and mobilize the notion
of medical neutrality to counter the state officials' criminalization
campaign against them. Then I analyze the moments and encounters in which the forensic and medical gaze falls short of addressing
the needs of people who were collectively revolting for democratic
rights and resisting state violence.

When the Gezi uprising erupted, I was volunteering at the
Human Rights Association and doing research at the Human Rights
Foundation of Turkey in Istanbul. The association was particularly
close to the main infirmary opened in the Taksim branch of the
Istanbul Medical Chamber. I helped bring medicine and people back
and forth between the association and the main infirmary. This gave
me the opportunity to observe the atmosphere of the infirmaries,

how fear and panic were enmeshed with excitement in these places. The Turkish Medical Association organized infirmaries and directed volunteer doctors and medical students to these sites of emergency care during the riots. It established the first infirmary in Taksim on June 1, the second day of the riots. This infirmary became the main center where doctors gathered, medical equipment was distributed, and mobile and temporary clinics were planned. At least ten mobile infirmaries at any one time were established each day in the side streets of Taksim where clashes took place. These infirmaries were run exclusively by volunteer doctors, nurses, paramedics, specialists, and medical students. Soon, the police forces began to harass these visible spaces of care.

I met Dr. Ayşe in one of the rooms of the foundation to hear the details of her experience during the Gezi uprising as a coordinator in one of the infirmaries established in a big store. She had worked as a volunteer at the Human Rights Foundation of Turkey for several years. What she remembered most vividly from those days was the police attack on the first infirmary while she was stitching a wound on a patient. The police even shot gas canisters inside and cut off the electricity. Anyone leaving the infirmary was beaten. Dr. Ayşe described those moments as follows: "There was too much noise. It was like a war zone. They destroyed all the equipment. We continued to establish new infirmaries, yet they kept attacking." Systematic use of tear gas, plastic bullets, water cannons, and pepper spray against the protestors and infirmaries continued in the following days. Another doctor who was a forensic medicine and public health specialist and took to the streets to protest the decision to demolish Gezi Park was Dr. Elmas. Immediately after, she realized that she was needed as a medical doctor. She remembers the moment when the police brutally dispersed the crowd she was part of in one of the narrow streets leading to Taksim Square. She continues, "As I was running away like everyone else from the tear gas or plastic bullets, I heard someone say, 'Is there a doctor around?' I stopped. I first hesitated. I knew I was risking my life by not running like the other protestors. But I also knew that I had to be there to treat the injured." As more and more protestors were injured and needed treatment, she just could not continue like a regular protestor and felt that she had to take up her medical identity. She was following the protestors even when she did not approve of their choice of action. The feeling that she had to help was "ingrained" in the training and practice of medicine. Her priority shifted from protecting the park to helping injured protestors. Despite the fact that she was sympathetic to demonstrators and sometimes wanted to participate, professional responsibilities prevented her from doing so in the following days as she sought to provide care for the protestors while in these mobile clinics. Doctors didn't feel completely passive in the face of these attacks. They aimed to circumvent police harassment by certain tactics including turning off the lights of infirmaries, closing their doors, and staying silent as the police forces passed by. As a rule, no single infirmary could stay for more than a day in the same location, flexibly moving to avoid police harassment and also to protect shop owners who did not want their workplaces to be associated with the already criminalized Gezi protestors.

By whom and to what ends medical care will be provided emerges as an important site of contention, especially in times of unrest and political conflict. The fact that doctors can assume different roles during political upheavals means that the neutrality of medical knowledge and care is not a given, but rather it is a site fraught with practical and ideological contention (Aciksoz 2015; Adams 1998; Redfield 2006). For example, in El Salvador health workers turned into radicalized actors drawing on the legitimacy and credibility of their profession to lead an important political and social change in the country (Smith-Nonini 2010). In Egypt, witnessing the deliberate targeting of doctors and field hospitals during the uprising transformed the political subjectivities of doctors (Hamdy and Bayoumi 2016). In a similar vein, many young doctors who volunteered in the Gezi infirmaries experienced this level of police violence for the first time in their lives. They were in the streets to help the protestors, but many of them did not think that they and their medical practice could be the target of police brutality. Even though the

atmosphere of the Gezi uprising was war-like at times, most protestors were unarmed citizens exercising their right to peaceful protest. Many of the young doctors had assumed that the principle of
non-interference with medical services in times of armed conflict
would be honored and would protect them from police violence.[5]
In addition to the use of force, the government started to put into
motion legal processes to criminalize the doctors and their alternative ethical frameworks. They sought to defame these doctors by
releasing fake news regarding the content of their medical practice
and by conducting legal investigations and passing a new bill concerning health care provision. This was most evident in the court
case involving allegations that Gezi doctors allowed people to enter
a mosque with their shoes on and consumed alcohol while treating injured protestors. The defenses of doctors during the court trial
revealed how they were forced to embody the forensic fantasies in
their narratives.

Criminalization of Doctors with Lawsuits and "Fake News"

When the police withdrew from Taksim Square on June 1, protests
shifted to other neighborhoods such as Beşiktaş, where the then
prime minister's office in İstanbul was located. Severe clashes took
place for three days around the vicinity of Dolmabahçe, where the
lack of shops and residential spaces forced doctors to turn the historical Dolmabahçe Mosque into an infirmary. The mosque infirmary
became emblematic as *the site* around which many government accusations against the Gezi protestors centered in the following months
and even years. Many representatives of the government publicly
announced explicit and implicit links between the provision of first
aid for the injured in the mosque and various acts of blasphemy
despite the absence of any visual or other kinds of evidence to prove
these acts. On June 11, 2013, during a parliamentary speech, the then
Prime Minister Erdoğan said: "You are going to enter the mosque

with your shoes on, you are going to drink alcohol and desecrate religious shrines of this country. All in the name of environment! You are going to threaten the muezzin[6] of the mosque so that he lies and says: Nothing like this has taken place. How can this happen? We have all the footage." (Hurriyet Daily News 2013) Neither the muezzin nor witnesses confirmed these accusations. The footage was never released. Doctors who worked at the Dolmabahçe Mosque infirmary stated that they were anxious about being there from the very beginning. They had assigned a person to take off the shoes of the injured. However, as things got out of control with violent police attacks in the area, it became almost impossible to make sure that everyone removed their shoes before they entered the mosque.

The government's defamation campaign had legal consequences. The Gezi indictment accepted by the court in December 2013 listed 255 defendants, and two of them were doctors who worked in the Dolmabahçe Mosque infirmary. The prosecutor noted that the doctors committed the crime of disrespecting sacred places and of protecting the "criminals" instead of turning them over to the police. Several medical and human rights associations—the Turkish Medical Association, the Human Rights Association, the Human Rights Foundation of Turkey, and the Society of Forensic Medicine Specialists—gathered in February 2014 to discuss the specifics of how to defend their colleagues, the honor of medical practice, and the universal values of medicine. One outcome was a press statement, before which Gezi doctors came together and discussed how to frame their position as doctors *and* pro-Gezi citizens.

In these debates, some doctors, especially younger ones, seemed hesitant about emphasizing the presumed neutrality of their professional identity to justify their actions during the Gezi protests, because this might, they felt, inadvertently delegitimize them. They felt uneasy about using their professional identity to rationalize their clinical practice to defend themselves during the trials that would deny their physical, emotional, and political proximity to the protestors. Despite these contentions, the final decision was to highlight medical-ethical principles in a statement. Ultimately, medical non-governmental organizations prepared a press statement and read it right in front of Dolmabahçe Mosque on April 2014. In it, they declared: "We said hundreds of times, whatever your laws, circulars, regulations say, we will continue to follow the universal principles of medical practice as we have been doing for thousands of years since Hippocrates."[7]

Dr. Can was one of the doctors tried for entering the mosque. He was an intern in the department of general medicine and was on duty for twenty-four hours at the hospital on the first day that the mosque was used as an infirmary. After trying many routes to get to his home that was close to where the clashes took place, he saw people who fainted or whose eyes and head were covered in blood and were running toward the mosque. Some people were carrying the injured to the mosque. During the trial, he said that as soon as he saw injured people, he immediately started to run toward the mosque with the "reflex of being a doctor." In the mosque, he helped establish a triage system to accurately identify those who needed the most urgent help. He continued: "It doesn't matter who the injured person is. Our professors at the medical school taught us that our mission is to treat everyone. If we hadn't intervened, many people could have died, some limbs could have been cut." Dr. Eren, a young medical doctor and a longtime volunteer for the Human Rights Foundation of Turkey, was the second doctor who was tried for disrespecting sacred places. She heard via social media that there was need for health care workers in the area as the number of injured people increased. So, she said, she felt she needed to go to the mosque because of the Hippocratic oath. She continued, "Over time the number of injured people and health care personnel increased in the mosque. There was a triage system. I called 112 [emergency call center in Turkey] many times for those in critical condition. Two or three ambulances arrived in an hour or so. If we weren't there, some people might have died." Her voice trembled when she denied the accusations of insulting religious values and damaging the mosque. "This cannot be our purpose. It was an emergency just like an earthquake, or flood. We acted with our professional reflex as we would do in times of other natural disasters. This is what we would do whenever we see an accident or a person who is having an attack." She concluded: "When I heard about the accusations about us, I was worried if I learned something wrong at the medical school. My professors are here. Please correct me if I'm wrong. At school we learned that if we hadn't done what we have done at the mosque, *that* would be a crime. This trial is not a requiem for Hippocrates but a eulogy for Hippocrates." These last words were clapped for a long time by the audience.

During the trials, doctors and their associations continued to rely on the universality and neutrality of medical practice and the idea of doctors' ethical responsibility for helping those who are in need. Their defense during these trials placed them in a separate position from the rest of the Gezi defendants as they explained their participation through their occupational ethics, not through citizens' constitutional right to hold "unarmed and peaceful meetings and demonstration marches without prior permission."[8] The primacy of the occupational ethics as the rationale for doctors' acts of solidarity during the Gezi uprising continued as the government kept targeting the content and scope of Gezi doctors' emergency-care work via a new legal regulation and a defamation campaign. On June 13, 2013, the minister of health announced a new bill to regulate emergency care, and the ministry lodged an official complaint against the Gezi doctors for providing illegal health services.[9] In order to create a legal base for this, the government officials did indeed later draft a bill that regulated emergency-care provision in January 2014. According to this bill, all practices and procedures related to the delivery of health services shall be under the scrutiny of the Ministry of Health. In emergency situations, "Until the arrival of formal health services, those who deliver or commission others to deliver health services without proper license shall be subject to imprisonment from one to three years and administrative fine equivalent to that of twenty thousand days [the fine is worth twenty thousand days of work]."[10] In order to find a rationale for introducing this bill, the Ministry of Health drew a very selective and partial picture of the health situation of the Gezi protesters and claimed that there were state hospitals and ambulances available for the injured. Various national and international medical associations found this bill extremely problematic (Physicians for Human Rights 2014). For example, the Turkish Medical Association declared that it was the nature of a medical crisis that should determine the need for emergency intervention, not the accessibility of a formal health service. Ambulances could not enter many areas where clashes took place because of the barricades. Sometimes ambulance drivers were afraid to go to the area, and, at times, they were blocked by police. For many doctors I interviewed, the bill primarily aimed to criminalize voluntary emergency medical care during the protests. Moving beyond the case of two doctors whose work at the mosque was tried, the bill wanted to bring all kinds of healthcare services under strict government control.

As part of the broader criminalization campaign, the Ministry of Health also aimed to restrict the selling of what it called "Gezi pharmaceuticals," namely the bundle of medicine used by protestors to protect themselves from the effects of tear and pepper gas. The police attacked Gezi Park on June 15, 2013, and confiscated all medicine in the main (informal) infirmary located in Gezi Park. Approximately nine months later, some pharmacists in Istanbul received an official letter from the Provincial Directorate of Health entitled "Regarding Gezi Park Pharmaceuticals" along with a list of pharmacies. The letter stated: "We would like to inform you that if your pharmacy continues to act in violation of the Regulation of Ministry of Health General Directorate for Pharmaceuticals and Pharmacy dated 31/11/2014 and numbered B10.0.İEG.0.73.00.17/89362 (2009/84), we will take criminal action against you." The Ministry of Health spent months trying to identify the origins of thousands of medical consumables and pharmaceuticals confiscated from the Gezi infirmaries through the Medicine Tracking System using 2D barcodes on pharmaceuticals. The government effectively used these confiscated pharmaceuticals to criminalize voluntary medical care during the Gezi uprising. To this end, the discourses deployed against the radical Left or Kurdish political organizations, especially in the 1990s, were recalled by the government and circulated again in television news and newspapers, this time targeting Gezi doctors, Gezi infirmaries, and mobile clinics. Pro-government media referred to infirmaries as "so-called," as they did with "terrorist" organizations: "the so-called leader/flag/member of terrorist organization PKK." "So-called" would discredit the doctors, their medical expertise, and practices.

The criminalization had a public and performative dimension. After receiving the pharmaceuticals from the Istanbul Police Headquarters and identifying and classifying them, the Health Directorate organized a press statement where "Gezi pharmaceuticals" were neatly placed on a table and labeled with name tags. The press was invited to take pictures and videos of these "Gezi pharmaceuticals,"[11] which include: Talcid, Gaviscon, Batticon, Benexol, Ventolin, and Antepsin. Medical consumables were also placed on the table, such as cotton, ethanol, rubber gloves, oxygen bottles, serum, and gauze bandage. For a generation who had witnessed police operations against "illegal revolutionary organizations," the practice of displaying "captured members of the organization" along with "captured organizational materials" such as "guns, explosives and bomb making materials" on the news was a familiar scene. Here, the familiar performative media genre used to criminalize political organizations was at work again, now criminalizing those who provided and used "Gezi pharmaceuticals."

All these initiatives of the government primarily aimed to curb the influence of progressive doctors and their associations with the younger generation of doctors and prevent the formation of solidarity networks between protestors and doctors. The Turkish Medical Association and its provincial branches, especially the Istanbul Medical Chamber, had requested doctors and medical students go to the protest areas to help the injured. To discuss the meaning and implications of these campaigns, I talked to Dr. Neslihan, one of the representatives of the Istanbul Medical Chamber who played an active role during the Gezi protests. She oversaw the organization of makeshift infirmaries and was closely following the lawsuits against doctors for helping the injured in the mosque. For her, there was no

question that the bill directly targeted the first aid units founded by
voluntary Gezi doctors. If providing emergency care was a crime,
Dr. Neslihan asked: "Why did the government let us help after the
earthquake in Van in 2011?" She then added: "The health situation
in Gezi was no different from what we would encounter in a natural
crisis situation, but it was a political one." Despite her emphasis on
the political nature of the Gezi protests, Dr. Neslihan also underlined
the continuities between natural disasters and political crises as far
as medical intervention is concerned: "We, as the Medical Association, called to doctors to join the medical teams, just like we would
do in other catastrophic situations. Hundreds of doctors responded
and volunteered. You might be against Gezi, but this cannot be a
reason to punish doctors for helping Gezi protestors."

All in all, the Gezi doctors' medical praxis had produced multiple
sites of contestation between doctors and the government. While doctors aimed to heal the injured during Gezi, the government mobilized
defamation campaigns and legal acts to criminalize their actions and
care practices, the pharmaceuticals they used, their medical records,
and their associations. In response, doctors that were put on trials
referred to articles in the Turkish Penal Code and the Convention on
Human Rights and Biomedicine that regulated the responsibilities of
doctors under emergency conditions. During the press conferences,
they also made use of rhetorical arguments: "If you want to put health
professionals on trial, you have to start with Hippocrates." By drawing on these legal protections as well as universal principles of medical ethics including the Hippocratic oath, doctors tried to render the
new legal regulations and the lawsuit illegitimate.

The more doctors resorted to professional principles, ethical
guidelines, and the Hippocratic oath when they were defending
their presence as medical experts during the protests, the more the
government used various legal, administrative, and performative
tools to delegitimize doctors' medical practices during these protests. One repercussion of this contention between the government
and medical workers was that even when doctors took to the streets
with political purposes, they ended up justifying their presence in

the streets with reference to ethical principles pertaining to medical care. In other words, the emphasis on their medical professional
identity gradually repressed their public political stance with respect
to the riots. The systematic efforts of criminalization and defamation in turn pushed these doctors toward a more strictly medical
discourse and ethical stance consolidating forensic fantasies as if
their political and collective identities are made up of their medical
witnessing to violence. Their initial enthusiasm about protecting the
park in Taksim Square and raising grievances about anti-democratic
practices that pulled them to the streets in the first days of protests
had weakened gradually, at least in their public discourses. Their
political desire for transformation remained in the background,
while their commitment to the medical profession and its binding
ethical principles that informed their medical interventions came to
the forefront.

Countering State Violence Through
Expert Witnessing

From the second day of the Gezi resistance, doctors working at the
infirmaries began to keep anonymous records of the number of
injured protestors, how they were injured, and what kind of treatment they received. "They [the government representatives] were
bothered by the fact that the events were being objectively reported
by doctors," said Ali Çerkezoğlu, the secretary general of the Istanbul Medical Association, to a reporter at the height of these clashes
(Associated Press 2014). As early as the first week of the Gezi uprising, the Human Rights Association made calls to all protesters asking them to visit medical institutions and provide medico-legal
reports to prove their bodily sufferings and injuries caused by police
violence. For example, the Turkish Medical Association made an
urgent call to start a web-based survey "in order to disclose the dangerous health effects of these gases targeted at defenseless people."
The findings were as follows: "In one week, over eleven thousand

people declared that they were affected by tear gas. Before the disaster on the 15th of June when the Gezi Park was attacked, the total number of injured people was 788 (7 percent). These data show that the police were targeting the people with riot gas. Many of the injuries we treated were on the head, face, eyes, thorax and abdomen, which could be fatal."[12]

Meanwhile, the Turkish Thoracic Society asked people to have their lungs tested to document the long-term effects of tear gas. Then, the Taksim Solidarity—a coalition consisting of approximately eighty organizations during the Gezi uprising including civil society groups, professional associations, political parties, and platforms— made a public announcement, asking people to visit their offices to recount to voluntary lawyers the different kinds of physical and psychological violations and violent acts to which they were subjected during the protests.[13] At the same time, in collaboration with various human rights and medical organizations, the Turkish Medical Association used the comprehensive data set they compiled on the public health consequences of police violence during the Gezi protests to expose state violence.[14] Similar to medical certificates testifying to torture on the individual body, these doctors were now documenting how the collective body of protestors were targeted by state violence. In response to these developments, the Ministry of Health sent an official letter to the Head of the Turkish Medical Association, asking for the names of the injured protestors treated at the temporary infirmaries and the names of the voluntary medical personnel. The association declined to give this information to the ministry on the grounds of patient-doctor confidentiality. Also, relying on this data, international organizations such as the World Medical Association, Doctors for Human Rights, the British Medical Association, and the German Medical Association condemned state violence in Turkey. Such documents were deemed crucial for filing complaints against the excessive use of police force at the ECHR.

On the eve of the Gezi trials in spring 2014, the doctors' campaign was announced with this slogan: "We are accusing *you*." The logic of this campaign goes like this: doctors not only provided medical treatment and emergency care for the injured in these infirmaries, but also documented the bodily consequences of police violence so that the latter could be proved and police could be prosecuted and future violence restricted. Thus, the injured body of the protestor would become the evidence of state violence through doctors' witnessing. It was their optimistic belief in the rehabilitative and recuperative power of their medical and forensic work that kept them doing what they were doing during the protests and afterward even when their work did not produce any concrete outcomes.

Medical humanitarian discourses and practices have increasingly resorted to bodily evidence as a primary venue for making claims when dealing with the refugee bodies in Europeans centers. For example, Ticktin (2011) discusses how the use of exceptional humanitarian measures, specifically the illness clause and verification via medical reports in the process of granting residency to immigrants in France, has had unintended political consequences. This purportedly apolitical regime of care sees the universal body as the ultimate "site of veracity" (Fassin 2012, 113) and reduces the applicant to his body and to his suffering. Many medical humanitarian practices are therefore criticized for translating "complex social processes . . . into the clinical language of human suffering" (Guilhot 2012, 90) in which the body of, say, a refugee or an asylum seeker emerges as the only source of authentic evidence, while their words become less and less important (Fassin 2012). When analyzing the bodily consequences of police violence during the Gezi uprising, doctors too relied on the concept of a universal, standardized body and followed the physical and psychological traces of violence on the body. Bodies were read as documents onto which state violence was inscribed. However, different from medical documents in European countries, these medical documents are not instruments for refugees to secure residency permits or other rights on medical humanitarian grounds. In the context of Turkey, these documents usually do not have any legal or practical consequences for the injured people. But they seem to have another function, which is to form new alliances against political violence between doctors, protestors, and non-governmental organizations against the excessive use of force by state officials. Gezi doctors and human rights organizations tried to circulate the idea that it was important to visit the Human Rights Foundation of Turkey or similar organizations to get protestors' suffering documented even when they did not expect that perpetrators would be punished. Thanks to their phantasmal investment in forensic medical documentation as a tool that would restrict the use of excessive force, they insisted on showing how and why excessive use of force should be considered torture. They wanted to convey this message to the larger sections of society with the help of their forensic-documentation practice. As a continuation of this strategy, progressive medical organizations continued to organize panels, forums, and symposia on the health consequences of the Gezi protests.

A symposium organized by seven non-governmental human rights and medical associations on January 25, 2014, approximately six months after the Gezi uprising, attests to doctors' commitment to forensic fantasies in times of Gezi. Titled "Torture in the Streets: Effects and Consequences of the Riot Control Agents," the symposium brought together medical and scientific knowledge accumulated during and after the Gezi protests regarding riot-control agents in a huge conference hall in a central district of Istanbul. All the presenters were experts in medicine or related fields (forensic medicine, toxicology, chemistry, chest and cardiovascular diseases, pharmacy, and psychiatry), and they gave presentations on the negative physical, social, and psychological consequences of the use of police force, especially that of tear gas, pepper gas, and plastic bullets during the Gezi protests. The hall was full, and everyone was listening to the presentations on Gezi's health toll with extreme attention. Mobilizing certain expert-witnessing techniques through data collection, testimony, and witnessing gathering (Givoni 2011, 2; Redfield 2006; Weizman 2012), these doctors showed the extent of police violence to delegitimize and reclassify excessive use of riot-control agents under the legal category of torture. Listening to the speakers was like listening to different stories about an incident one lived. Most debates at the symposium questioned to what extent and in which ways the use of tear gas could be classified as torture. Drawing on scientific and medical expertise, most presenters argued that the use of tear gas can and should be classified as torture and therefore be banned. There were also debates around if the use of tear gas could be proven; how it impacted lungs, orientation, and eyes; and how these bodily consequences were often not proportionate with the necessary level of violence to contain the riot. Legal experts on the panel also made references to the ECHR's decision that classifies excessive, intensive, or disproportionate use of tear gas as torture and ill treatment. Drawing on the information provided by medical experts, they underlined the fact that the suffering caused by tear gas could be traumatic because it was inflicted by human-beings and it was systematic. Medical and legal experts frequently high-lighted how these were the two defining characteristics of the legal definition of torture in the Turkish criminal code.

At the end of the day, most speakers and people in the audience seemed to have agreed on the fact that tear gas was a form of torture, and it was the task of medical experts in the field of human rights to constantly search for ways of demonstrating how excessive use of tear gas and pepper spray amounted to torture. This seeming con-sensual atmosphere was challenged during the discussion session. One psychiatrist, whom I have known from his volunteer work at the Human Rights Foundation of Turkey, underscored the risk of using the term torture to account for all kinds of police violence and people's experience of it without really making a distinction between the two groups' understanding of the word. He pointed to the poster of the symposium that hung behind the stage. It was a picture of a young man surrounded by tear gas smoke. He was about to run away while kicking against a tear gas canister thrown at him and other protestors. He did not look passive or desperate at all. On the contrary, there was an excitement in his bodily movements. So, the psychiatrist said, "I don't see a person under torture in this picture. When attacked with tear gas, people during the Gezi were singing back at the police 'c'mon spray pepper gas/c'mon take off your mask and drop your batons/let's see who a real man is!' They were not afraid of the police." For him, collective action and voice during the protest empowered those who were subjected to violence in the public sphere. In that sense, he believed that their stress on bodily suffering in fact carried the risk of rendering this empowerment invisible.

This tension between the desire to prove violence through the injured body and the feeling of empowerment that comes with the resistance could be observed in the reports and statements prepared by the doctors at the Human Rights Foundation of Turkey. For example, the foundation prepared a detailed report that consists of medical evaluations of the applicants who visited the foundation in June and July of 2013, the period when most of the clashes took place. The report evidences the scale and extent of the use of demonstration-control agents during the protests in the weeks following the Gezi uprising through a medical evaluation of 297 cases. The report further discusses how and why the stories of police violence told by applicants are consistent with the scars that doctors detected on their bodies. After summarizing and classifying the most widespread methods of torture used by the police during and after the riots, this Gezi report by the foundation ends with a cautionary note that highlights the limitations of the report in grasping the mood of collective solidarity enabled by the Gezi uprising and how it partly undoes the potentially harmful psychological consequences of torture.

This report and the doctors that I talked to about Gezi highlighted that the collective spirit of the riot helped many victims of violence to go through the processes of post-violence without necessarily feeling traumatized. On the contrary, these sources note that most of the applicants mentioned how they felt animated and spiritually enriched thanks to the solidarity and hope of the Gezi uprising. In other words, the experience of solidarity operated as a positive and protective influence on the mental states of those who were subjected to violence. As one of the doctors that I talked to noted, "Gezi gave us hope as much as pain."

Previous chapters have demonstrated how the forensic fantasies kept doctors who were fighting for human rights in Turkey in the field of documentation of human rights violations against all odds.

The Gezi protests threw these fantasies into sharp relief because police violence and resistance against violence during the Gezi protests do not easily fit into the classical torture experience where the victim is alone and vulnerable in the presence of the police. To begin with, Gezi doctors' provision of emergency health care has features such as physical and emotional proximity to the injured at the time of the event and the impossibility of securing safe zones to provide emergency care due to the police attack on doctors. This resulted in the systematic criminalization and defamation of doctors during and after the Gezi protests. In turn, doctors referred to a medical neutrality that entails forensic fantasies as a way to account for their presence in the field. This humanitarian perspective has had repercussions for how these doctors perceived the protest. Doctors' experiences with the injured protestors during and after the Gezi protests truly show the limits of their forensic fantasies in terms of how they restrict political imagination by seeking to translate it into the language of legal compensation and punishment. The failure to grasp the broader political truth of people's resistance (vis-à-vis the notions of collectivity, solidarity, and hope) thus also reveals the limits of humanitarian and human rights discourses that prioritize the medical gaze and the scientific truth of state violence.

The Limits of Political
Fantasies and Evidence

Du-
ring my research in 2012 and 2013, doctors, political activists, and lawyers in the field of human rights told me that "older" or "classical" forms of torture, such as falanga or electric shock, were no longer used in police stations. Other practices that did not quite sound like torture had replaced them: the police would tighten plastic handcuffs too hard to hurt the wrists of detainees; use batons, tear gas, or pepper spray against peaceful protestors; or keep detainees in extremely hot or cold police buses for many hours. Doctors fighting for human rights argued that these acts should be classified as torture or ill-treatment if they are disproportional and violate human dignity. These doctors' affective and political commitment to uncovering the truth about police violence formed the core of their forensic fantasies.

Soon after I ended my research, I began to observe that the ground upon which these forensic fantasies were built was gradually transforming. In the aftermath of the failed coup attempt by an Islamist faction of the Turkish Armed Forces against the government in July 2016, the government declared a state of emergency and started to rule the country with executive orders, evoking what Naomi Klein (2007) would call the "shock doctrine." The public visibility of state violence increased unapologetically from then on.[1] The escalation in military clashes in Kurdish cities after the collapse of a temporary

ceasefire between the PKK and the Turkish army in 2016 accentu-
ated the graphic depiction of violence by security forces in photographs and video clips. Alongside these violent events and the trend
of normalizing excessive and illegal violence against "dissident"
groups, Turkey's EU accession process was rapidly withering, caus-
ing the political decay of the principles of democracy and human
rights. What happens to the status of medical evidence and forensic
fantasies in this new paradigm? How can we understand this transformation within the broader global context?

The widespread circulation of photographs of tortured bodies in
pain and suffering has become a manifestation of power through
what Foucault calls "punishment-as-spectacle." There has also been
a shift in the work of these documents in this context. Rather than
simply being visual and evidential documents of violent acts, they
have become instruments of state violence.[2] During this turn toward
authoritarianism and securitization in the country, a trend recog-
nizable globally, we have also witnessed the collapse of the regime
of denial alongside the normalization of the public spectacle of state
violence in Turkey. In other words, how security forces or state officials engage with questions of evidence of violence in Turkey has
also begun to change. State officials seemed less compelled to deny
or exceptionalize these acts of disproportionate uses of force or to
try to cover them up as they did in the 1980s and 1990s, ignoring
and undermining democratic publics that expected responsible
action from the state.[3] Moreover, different from state officials in the
1990s, state officials now seem intent on mobilizing all available legal
mechanisms to render their violent acts legally justified, raising the
acceptable level of state violence in favor of the state. Once members
of the army and police forces become accustomed to acting violently
with political impunity under the protection and mandate of new
legal reforms and government policies, there is a significant risk
of the use of punishment as spectacle whenever they encounter a
potential "terrorist" threat. It is the biopolitical sanctity of life that
sustains the logic of security and normalizes the torture or killing of
the "terrorist." Torture involves the deliberate infliction of physical

or psychological harm on individuals in custody who have not been convicted of a crime. Torture is considered an extralegal practice, as it does not include harms resulting from court-ordered punishments that align with a country's criminal laws. Yet, what we have been observing is the proliferation of the procedures, regulations, and mechanisms that normalize and legitimize why a particular act of violence was necessary, proportionate, and therefore legal in response to a particular threat to the society.

The government officials had nothing to hide or deny as a consequence of the biopolitical logic of anti-terror laws that were enacted in accordance with the securitization logic prevalent in EU countries. Sophisticated and flexible legal framework could be used to legitimize sovereign violence of the state. These laws enabled the state to inflict violence on potential terrorist suspects as long as these acts aim to protect the larger social body. This logic was inscribed with the help of legislative changes at the international level as well. For example, those who were negatively affected by the curfews during the clashes submitted petitions to the Constitutional Court and the ECHR to overturn curfew declarations. The ECHR dismissed the application and evoked the biopolitical logic by saying that "the court relies on the [Turkish] government to take any necessary steps to ensure that physically vulnerable individuals can have access to treatment if they so request."[4] We are seeing an increasing number of cases where the office of the governor or the Ministry of Justice would not permit legal investigation of torture allegations on grounds that the violence was proportionate.[5] Which acts of state officials are or can be considered torture is always a contested subject, and the scope of these debates often takes place against the backdrop of broader historical transformations in technologies of state violence, global trends in human rights movements, and intranational political struggles.

The global war on terror and the global normalization and routinization of state violence after 9/11 was a critical turning point for torture debates everywhere (Hopgood, Snyder, and Vinjamuri 2018). The circulation of photographs depicting the excessive acts of security forces brought into question the status of enhanced interrogation techniques in black sites run by the United States and Israel. State power has been expanding at the expense of human rights (Hopgood 2013). Human rights practitioners and civil rights advocates have argued that no cause or crisis justifies disregarding the absolute prohibition of torture. The underlying principle that has informed different anti-torture movements across the globe is the prohibition of torture is absolute; everyone, everywhere, and under all circumstances has the right not to be tortured. Lisa Hajjar proposes that we can understand the problem of torture as "sovereign states transgressing sovereign bodies for whatever security or political reasons drive custodial abuse in any given context" (Hajjar 2022, 5). The right not to be tortured is the most universal right and is protected by national and international laws.

There has been extensive critical research on exceptional and excessive forms of violence in the form of enhanced interrogation techniques taking place in Abu Ghraib, Guantanamo, and Israeli detention centers. However, we need more research on how everyday forms of policing are changing and transforming the field for human rights activism in specific contexts. Everyday policing—as opposed to the more spectacular police interventions that proliferate in the media—occurs at a time when the police are becoming more repressive, and penalties are becoming severer across the democracies of Europe and North America. Recent ethnographies of policing (Yonucu 2022; Ralph 2020; Fassin 2013) show in different ways how both ordinary and extraordinary forms of police force are used to maintain a particular social order, which reproduces sections of the population who are seen as threatening by virtue of their mere existence—that is, young people from working-class neighborhoods, mostly belonging to minorities—regardless of any objective danger. Ordinary police work involves aggressive and humiliating treatment in a context where exceptional police measures have been legitimized, increasing disorder and insecurity, especially for undocumented migrants, drug users, and political dissidents. Undoubtedly, certain marked populations and dissidents are more likely to become the object of these types of mundane forms of state violence, which do not aim at killing but leave psychological and physical scars on individuals.

When investigating the less visible consequences of anti-Black police violence, Puar calls this the state's "right to maim" and defines it as a strategy to undermine, disable, or manage dissident or insurgent groups and to create living deaths. While Puar's (2017) illuminating discussion reveals the extent of these issues, this research traces the medico-legal consequences of these regimes of injury and debilitation within the bureaucratic and legal frameworks of existing democratic systems, focusing on the subjectivities of doctors. It is the work of doctors trained in the public health tradition that have been forming a protective shelter around these injured bodies. Wendy Brown has long warned about the limitations of the politics of rights. The latter might shield subjects from state coercion, yet they do not diminish the power of the state (Brown 1995). Brown further adds that "Yes, the abuse must be stopped but by whom, with what techniques, with what unintended effects, and above all, unfolding what possible futures?" (Brown 2004, 460). While understanding her critique of human rights discourse and its tendency to be "pragmatist, moral, and antipolitical," I also maintain that there is more to human rights activism. Following Babül's suggestion that despite liberalization and bureaucratization of human rights rhetoric in the post–Cold War period, "the particular political path of human rights in Turkey produced less streamlined, more complex results," (Babül 2020), I argue that doctors who have aligned themselves with human rights principles imagine their medical witnessing work as a radical political practice that has transformative power vis-à-vis state violence. Their practice has a strong affective and ideological dimension that ensures that their political and collective identities are formed collectively and stay consistent for decades.

Today we are at a crossroads regarding the future of human rights projects around the globe. Peacebuilding projects and transitional justice mechanisms no longer enjoy their previous broad-based popularity or legitimacy. Government representatives everywhere seem less interested in reckoning with and not quite willing to face the past state crimes they are accused of. When punishment as spectacle becomes widespread in society and normalized by higher state authorities under the protection and mandate of legal reforms, the relevance of medical or forensic medicine for creating evidence or counterevidence of torture becomes less effective. Accordingly, the consensus among human rights activists, state officials, political groups, and victims of violence on the importance of uncovering the truth about past state crimes and the idea that the truth could lead to a more peaceful and democratic future seems to be withering away, if not completely disappearing. Yet, despite this global rise of right-wing authoritarianisms, national and international non-governmental organizations and political actors continue to deploy sophisticated forensic technologies and expertise to detect evidence of state crimes and share it in multiple forms such as documents, video clips, photographs, digital visualizations, and recordings. Despite the overabundance of evidence of violence produced by civil society organizations, their political and legal efficacy in bringing about progressive change by restricting state violence, healing past wounds, or building peace is weak. The notion of forensic fantasy helps us understand the fundamental tension of our contemporary moment of post-truth.

The aftermath of violence often creates a post-factual landscape (Nichanian 2009; Cohen 2001; Taussig 1984) that makes it impossible to prove the intention or will behind state violence. In our post-truth era, one reason people are anxious about the breakdown of consensus about the facts and the erosion of scientific authority is the difficulty of imagining a collective horizon in the absence of collective truths. My research sheds light on these anxieties and argues that facts in and of themselves will not rescue us from this crisis. An ethnographic reflection on recent debates on post-truth through the question of political violence highlights the malleability of facts (especially medical and scientific ones) and their limited power in naming state violence and restoring justice in the aftermath of violence. Forensic and medical documentation of violence can be easily stuck in an endless dialogue and contention regarding the determination of facts and evidence around the logic of proof and denial.

However, it is the fantasy of forensics that takes these doctors out of this loop. By holding on to their political identities and expert communities via forensic fantasies, these doctors are not stuck in the logic of proof and denial. Their affective and ethical commitment to the work they do, their constant dialogue and trust-filled relationship with political groups and victims of state violence, and, finally, their love for other members of this community keep them motivated and creative as they continue to produce the truth of violence even if their findings tend to lose their evidential relevance in the legal and administrative fields while extreme forms of violence by security forces are tolerated by politicians.

NOTES

Introduction

1. For the full text of Article 94 in 5237 Turkish Criminal Law, see: https://www.mevzuat.gov.tr/mevzuat?MevzuatNo=5237&MevzuatTur=1& MevzuatTertip=5.

2. The convention is available at https://www.ohchr.org/en/instruments -mechanisms/instruments/convention-against-torture-and-other-cruel -inhuman-or-degrading.

3. Article 16 is available at https://www.mevzuat.gov.tr/mevzuat?Mevzuat No=2559&MevzuatTur=1&MevzuatTertip=3. Emphasis mine.

4. After the coup, many international organizations criticized the representatives of the government for tolerating systematic and widespread use of torture against the ideological and ethnic others of the country. Amnesty International's report *Turkey: Testimony on Torture* (Amnesty International 1985) is one of the first documents that explicitly state that torture was widespread and systematic in Turkey in the post-1980 coup period. The report draws on testimonies of torture survivors, interviews with former political prisoners, and letters from political refugees, as well as newspaper articles. Later, Human Rights Foundation of Turkey also prepared a comprehensive report on the prevalence of torture throughout the 1990s entitled *İşkence Dosyası: Gözaltında ya da Cezaevide Ölenler 12 Eylül 1980–12 Eylül 1995* (Torture File: Deaths Under Custody or in Prison 12 September 1980–12 September 1995). Also see Tuşalp 1986 for more stories on torture in the post-1980 period and Yıldız and McDermott 2004 for a trajectory of torture cases between 1980 and 2000 with an emphasis on how torture was used during the Kurdish conflict. Despite the fact that the above-mentioned reports and books mostly rely on torture experiences of political activists, I should add that anyone who interacted with the security forces in police stations and prisons, especially members of oppressed and marginalized groups (thieves, beggars,

street children, LGBTI individuals, etc.), were under the high risk of being subjected to classical forms of torture in the 1980s and 1990s.

5. The most comprehensive data on the transformation of political violence in Turkey since the 1990s can be found in the annual reports of the Human Rights Foundation of Turkey. See https://tihv.org.tr/yillik-insan-haklari-raporlari/.

6. Torture in the 2000s was best documented in Pişkinsüt's (2001) book *Filistin Askısından Fezlekeye İşkencenin Kitabı* (*The Book of Torture: From Palestine Hanging to Police Report*). This book draws on observations and interviews Pişkinsüt and her team conducted in police stations when she was the chairwoman of the Human Rights Commission of Turkish National Grand Assembly.

Chapter 1

1. Hunger strikes were the most widely used form of resistance among political prisoners in the aftermath of the coup.

2. These two names also appeared among the 1,650 officials who were investigated during the September 12 trials that started in 2012. Even though the court gave life sentences to two military commanders that led to the coup, their sentences were not approved by the Supreme Court because both convicts passed away during the trials.

3. Sadık Güleç. 2021. "CIA'den SADAT'a: Özel Harp Taktikleri." *Gazete Duvar*, October 30, 2021. https://www.gazeteduvar.com.tr/ciaden-sadata-ozel-harp-taktikleri-haber-1540080.

4. T24. 2011. "Küçükizsiz: O Mamak'ın Mengele's ydi." *T24*, November 13, https://t24.com.tr/haber/kucukizsiz-o-mamakin-mengelesiydi,181220.

5. As opposed to these doctors, Soyer also gave examples of doctors who were accused of providing treatment for the political dissidents or guerillas, especially in the Kurdish region.

6. The most important recent document in that regard is the official report prepared by the State Supervisory Council upon the request of the president of the republic in 2010. The full version of the report was never released, but even the summary was very critical of the workings of the CFM. The summary is available at http://www.tccb.gov.tr/ddk/.

7. This phrase was commonly used as a cover when political activists were extrajudicially killed by the police.

8. Besides talking to the family members of Süleyman Cihan, for this section I also benefited from the book *Süleyman Cihan: The Life of a Communist Leader*, prepared by Süleyman Cihan's brother Ahmet Cihan, who is a lawyer,

and Mehmet Çetin in 2011. This book is a compendium of all official documents regarding the detention and death of Süleyman Cihan under torture, including correspondences between different state institutions such as the military court, the anti-terror police, the CFM, and the lawyers of the family at the time of the incident and afterward.

9. See the related articles on the alternative report: http://www.bianet .org/bianet/insan-haklari/142898-savcinin-agar-ve-sahin-i-sorusturmaya -yetkisi-yok-mu and http://www.etha.com.tr/Haber/2012/04/21/guncel/iste -suleyman-cihan-cinayetinin-failleri/.

10. He is talking about the right of a family to bring their lawyer or expert witness to the autopsy investigation.

11. The book prepared by the US-based international non-governmental organization Physicians for Human Rights (1996) entitled *Torture in Turkey & Its Unwilling Accomplices: The Scope of State Persecution and the Coercion of Physicians* also points out this curious situation regarding doctors' report-writing practices in Turkey. Based on interviews with seventy-six health professionals between June 1994 and October 1995, the authors make the observation that in many cases doctors refrain from examining the detainee or reporting the findings due to police presence in the examination room or government coercion of health professionals. The authors further argue that even when the doctors "report physical findings, they do not draw any reasonable medical inference that the likely cause of the symptoms and signs was due to torture" (PHR 1996, 6). Even though the research was conducted with doctors working in different hospitals, it gives an important insight about the dominant report-writing tradition in Turkey. Inferring the cause of a particular scar and claiming that the scar was the result of torture would mean destroying the *scientific neutrality* of the profession in general and that of the medical document in particular.

Chapter 2

1. Dr. Ozden did not put her signature on the report because she had not completed her mandatory service and did not receive her official diploma yet. Dr. Fincancı did not put her signature on the report either on the grounds that it might lead to the conflict of interest as she was also working in the CFM at the time. Immediately after this incident, however, she was fired from the council.

2. The details of the case are available at https://www.hurriyet.com.tr /gundem/yargitaydan-polise-iskence-uyarisi-38437810.

3. The post-coup period was underlined by several political and economic changes: massive violation of human rights in the prisons, rise of

armed Kurdish guerrilla movement, transition from the import substitution industrialization to the export-oriented neoliberal economic model, privatization of state enterprises, and explosion of consumption culture along with the awakening of new modern desires for the larger segments of population. During this period, social and economic inequalities were restructured in such a way to redraw the lines between what is normal and what is deviant and between who is worthy, who is less worthy, and who is worthless. I thus approach the coup as a rupture in the ways people conceive their and others' bodies and the worthiness of these bodies. Large sections of the society, especially those that were associated with radical social movements of the 1970s were cast as terrorist or anarchist. However, despite systematic criminalization of people who were affiliated with radical social movements, they continued to maintain organic ties with certain sections of the society, including doctors who have sympathy either for oppressed groups or for leftist or Kurdish radical political movements.

4. That is, along with the decline of radical or sectarian political ideology, the diffusion of a language of rights and justice in the political sphere has taken place. This, however, did not lead to the disappearance of the radical leftist and Kurdish movements that use violence or are tolerant toward the use of physical violence for political purposes. They maintained their place on the list of threats to the national security of the Republic of Turkey. These organizations were "illegal" in the eyes of the state not only because they were challenging the sovereignty of the state but also because they had a claim to an alternative sovereignty. See Bargu (2014b) for a critical analysis of radical leftist history with a focus on the question of sovereignty.

5. Torture or torturing someone to death are often considered power techniques of a premodern era because the legitimacy of the modern state is assumed to lie in its capacity to sustain life, not in its sovereign power over death (Foucault 1978). It is considered "uncivilized" to inflict "physical pain" (Asad 1997, 289), and torture should be "condemned" in a modern and civilized state.

6. Dr. Leyla, who greeted me at the foundation, even told me that we could do collaborative research and publish together. I soon realized that she thought I was going to need numbers and statistics regarding the torture cases they documented. I told her that I might use numbers, but my research was going to be about doctors who are firsthand witnesses to violence in various clinical settings, including the doctors from the foundation.

7. It is in such constellations that evidence can be contested with counter-interpretations (Keenan and Steyerl 2014) because evidence is never evident. As argued, evidence is rather about making truthful or factual claims that

are persuasive and thus need to be interpreted to become evident (Csordas 2004, 475). Accordingly, neither forensic evidence nor forensic expertise are given. They are rather things that people do and practices they engage in, and all these practices yield intimacies of sorts. If we place evidence in its context of emergence and use, we see that the medical-expert witnessing is always an expertise-in-practice that can be observed and analyzed only in the real-time interaction.

8. Dr. Fincancı was sentenced to two years and six months in prison for signing the infamous peace petition to stop clashes in the Kurdish region and stayed in prison for ten days before she was released upon her lawyers' objection in 2018. In 2019, upon rumors that her acquittal could be overturned by the higher court and she might be dismissed from her position at the university, she decided to retire. She was in a sense forced to retire by legal means.

9. The activities of the Turkish Medical Association were suspended between 1980 and 1982 after the coup d'état.

10. While the former declaration is on the rights of the patient, the latter postulates "guidelines for physicians concerning torture and other cruel, inhuman or degrading treatment or punishment in relation to detention and imprisonment."

11. Dr. Nusret Fişek's defense at the court and his anti–capital punishment activism played an important role in preventing the implementation of this punishment. He also lobbied for national medical professional ethics regulation in accordance with human rights principles. The details of his achievements can be found in this article written by his son, who is also a professor of medicine: Gürhan Fişek. 2011. "Prof. Dr. Nusret H. Fişek: Bir Önderin Seyir Defteri." *Halk Sağlığında Gündem Bülteni*, Kasım 2011, https://nusret.fisek.org.tr/onun-icin-yazdilar/dr-a-gurhan-fisek/.

12. Dr. Şebnem Korur Fincancı called him the "stem cell" (*kök hücre*) of the doctors' human rights movement during her emotional and political retirement speech on the campus of Istanbul University in January 2019.

13. It was easier for activists to engage in public forms of politics in these cities compared to Kurdish region where the actions of security forces were unrestrained and political activities in the public space were far more restricted due to the ongoing state of emergency rule in the region.

14. These dignified stories of torture resistance were very much in circulation before the coup and continued to be formative for dissident personality in the aftermath of the 1980 coup d'état as well.

15. Dr. Soyer, another important public health figure, explicitly reflected on how doctors should approach the question of state violence. He was a follower of

Dr. Nusret Fişek and worked actively at the Ankara Medical Chamber. Despite highlighting the responsibilities of doctors in the face of torture, he also developed a concise and early critique of the risk of medicalizing torture documentation. According to Dr. Soyer, doctors should go beyond biomedical approaches that strictly focus on the individual health consequences of torture. Even in his early writings on the issue, he distanced himself from a particular medicalized approach to torture: "The impact of torture is immediately visible in the form of individual illnesses that are isolated from the larger societal context. However, this medicalized approach highlights torture as a private and individual experience. The suffering of the tortured individual is explained with psychiatric concepts. Then the 'rehabilitation' process follows" (Soyer 1993, 107).

16. The doctors of the Human Rights Foundation of Turkey prefer to use the term applicant instead of patient, victim, or activist to describe a person who visits their offices to receive medical treatment or medical reports regarding their injuries.

17. This two-page document is available at the archives of the Istanbul branch of the Human Rights Association.

18. To convincingly make the argument that the state does not tolerate torture, it incorporated the logic of a healthiness report by introducing an amendment in the "Regulation on Apprehension, Detention and Statement Taking" in 1998. According to this regulation, which will be detailed in the Chapter 3, the police are required to take detainees to a medical examination before and after detention. Moreover, this examination should take place within the scope of the patient-doctor relationship. This regulation has two aims: to protect the detainee from undue police violence under custody and to protect the police from torture allegations.

19. Another product of this forensic aesthetic is the illustrated "Atlas of Torture: Use of Medical and Diagnostic Examination Results in the Medical Assessment of Torture" (Özkalıpçı et al. 2010) where the bodily consequences of each method of torture are shown with pictures. Both these tools are considered indispensable for rehabilitation, diagnosis, and documentation of torture.

20. TİHV-HRFT Report. 2011. "People Tortured in Turkey from age 5 to 70." *Bianet*, July 12, 2011. https://bianet.org/english/human-rights/247117-people-tortured-in-turkey-from-age-5-to-70.

Chapter 3

1. He had certain limitations in cognitive functioning and skills.

2. NTV Haber. 2012. "Polise Hastanede Dayak." *NTV*, August 7, 2012. https://www.ntv.com.tr/turkiye/polise-hastanede-dayak,QasCijIy802AlD38

YhT3MA. The footage of the beatings at the police station was revealed by a reporter four months later and broadcasted with the title: "Bir polis dayağının öncesi ve Sonrası" ("Before and After of a Police Beating") and "Aile Boyu Dayak" ("Family Size Beating"). See http://webtv.radikal.com.tr/Turkiye/2242/bir-polis-dayaginin-oncesi-ve-sonrasi.aspx.

3. The public announcement of the Human Rights Association regarding this press statement is dated August 22, 2012 and titled "To the Attention of Press: Torture in Police Stations."

4. Neither this incident nor the press statement above is unique or rare. On the contrary, as traditional methods of torture such as falanga and Palestinian suspension have been eliminated from police stations in the last decade, beatings inside and outside of the police stations and in police cars have increased (Göregenli and Özer 2010). During my fieldwork at the Human Rights Association, each week there would be at least one or two applications for legal and medical assistance in the face of police violence. Legal aid is provided by the volunteer lawyers of the association. They are then directed to the Human Rights Foundation of Turkey for medical treatment and documentation.

5. In some cases, these reports are used as evidence to file countersuits against the victims of torture. This tendency was documented in the reports of the Human Rights Foundation of Turkey.

6. The journey of this progressive article regarding a detainee's health continued in the first half of the 2000s when Turkey's EU candidacy was on top of the government's political agenda. State officials would rush to find ways to comply with the requirements of the EU membership, including human rights principles. During these years, the ECHR also found the Turkish government guilty of not properly investigating and preventing torture cases and thus violating the right to life. In response, the government sought to strengthen mechanisms to prevent and document torture. As a result, Article 9 was amended in 2005 to link the documentation of a detainee's health to torture. Most notably, the amended version empowered the position of doctors vis-à-vis the police by putting the former in touch with prosecutors by stating that if the doctor detected any evidence that suggested crimes of torture, severe torture, or torment took place under custody, then they had to notify the public prosecutor immediately. A detainee's body was now considered forensic evidence to study, analyze, and document the culpability of state officials regarding the use of undue violence.

7. The regulation respects the privilege of doctors and detainees/patients by stating that the "doctor and the person who is being examined should be alone and examination should take place within the framework of

doctor-patient relationship are fundamental to examination." Although the doctor was given the chance to request to conduct the examination under the supervision of a law enforcement officer if they had fears regarding personal security, the detainee was first and foremost framed as a patient in the eye of the law makers. The article further stipulated that the law enforcement officer bringing the detainee before a doctor for medical examination should not be the same individual conducting the interrogation. This meant that police officers who were likely to have committed disproportionate violence would not be with the detainee as they were visiting the doctor. The regulation ideally protected not only the detainee against police brutality with the threat of documentation, but also the police against false accusations of torture.

8. The full title of the Trilateral Protocol is the Protocol on the Management of Prisons and Detention Houses, External Protection, Dispatch and Transport and Implementation of Health Services of the Convicts and Prisons.

9. This protocol is a set of international guidelines for "the assessment of persons who allege torture and ill-treatment, for investigating cases of alleged torture, and for reporting such findings to the judiciary and any other investigative body."

10. Instructors highlighted that the principles stipulated by the Istanbul Protocol were based on the universal principles of medical ethics and therefore binding for doctors. National regulations and instructions that are in contradiction with the protocol can be declared null according to the hierarchy of norms.

11. That is, thanks to these procedural guarantees, official doctors produce all this data in the form of medical reports in public hospitals.

12. The police might ask for two types of reports depending on whether a detainee is taken into custody or released from custody: entry or exist reports (*Giriş ve çıkış raporları*). If the detention period is extended, the police have to get another round of reports for extension purposes.

13. Here I follow Joan Scott's use of the term "echo." As an imperfect return of sound, Scott (2012) uses the analytics of fantasy echo to historically expand our horizon for the diverse possibilities of political and social identification through fantasy.

14. However, as we have seen, the detainee/patient does not always respond with a "no" and in some cases insists on being examined by the doctor.

Chapter 4

1. See "Öcalan: Hasta tutuklular rehine olarak tutuluyor," *Mezopotamya Ajansı*, September 7, 2021. http://mezopotamyaajansi35.com/tum-haberler/content/view/145876.

2. It is also true that if the government were to let hundreds of prisoners die in prison cells, prisons could turn into sites of collective anger and grief due to such politicized deaths. See Leshem, "'Over Our Dead Bodies': Placing Necropolitical Activism"; Bargu, "Another Necropolitics."

3. Namely these groups were the Revolutionary People's Liberation Party Front, the Communist Party of Turkey (Marxist Leninist), the Workers' Peasants' Liberation Army of Turkey, and the Communist Workers' Party of Turkey.

4. See the parliamentary question no. 7/5719, 12/3/2002.

5. This syndrome is "characterized by the presence of a triad of symptoms: ocular disturbances (ophthalmoplegia), changes in mental state (dementia), unsteady stance and gait (ataxia)." See http://en.wikipedia.org/wiki/Wernicke %E2%80%93Korsakoff_syndrome.

6. Ahmet Necdet Sezer, the then president of the republic, pardoned more than 181 political prisoners who suffered from Wernicke-Korsakoff syndrome between 2001 and 2006. See the parliamentary question no. 7/13337, 12/05/20106.

7. Only 51 of 614 people had these illnesses during the hunger strike protests that took place prior to 2001. The rest suffered this syndrome during the last wave of the hunger strike that started in 2000.

8. Many of the prisoners applied to the Human Rights Foundation of Turkey for treatment and rehabilitation after their release. The foundation was overwhelmed by the demand and mobilized a vast network of volunteer doctors from many different specialties. These doctors either came to the Taksim office of the foundation to meet the patients or accepted them in the hospitals that they were working at.

9. The research in the archives of *Milliyet Daily Newspaper* shows that there was almost no public discussion regarding the use of Article 399 before 2000, and it is rare for a court to rule on the postponement of execution of a sentence.

10. The radical political parties who organized the hunger strike were furious about the government's release policy. To them, the government sought to break the resistance through this policy. A member of one such party stated in the months following the first wave of releases: "We are witnessing something that an oligarchy would never do under normal conditions. Tens of prisoners, not only those who are disabled but also those who carry out a hunger strike, are being released." An anonymous article entitled "Releases: How to Ruin the Game? How to Be an Instrument to the Game" was published in 2001 in *Vatan*, a journal published by one of the radical leftist groups that carried out the hunger strike. The article is available at: http://www.ozgurluk.info/kitaplik /webarsiv/vatan/vatan99/tahliye.html.

11. The policy changes can rather be traced through some official figures that occupy important bureaucratic positions in medical or legal institutions. These figures act on behalf of what they call "the interests of the state," i.e. an abstraction they use to justify their acts. The continuity effects of state institutions are maintained through these figures who claim to act and talk on behalf of the name and interest of the state. One of these figures is Ali Suat Ertosun, who was the head of the General Directorate for Punishment and Prisons in 2000. It is rumored that he visited one of the doctors at CFM just before the preparation of the first wave of official medical certificates, which was the basis for the release of the hunger strikers.

12. The rest of the statement is available at http://istanbul.indymedia.org/en/news/2003/12/4063.php.

13. Bianet. 2004. "TİHV: Adli Tıp Kurumu Özerk Olmalı," *Bianet*, March 19, 2004. http://bianet.org/bianet/siyaset/31378-tihv-adli-tip-kurumu-ozerk-olmali.

14. See the relevant article from the year 2004 published in the *Radical Daily*: http://www.radikal.com.tr/veriler/2004/07/31/haber_123698.php.

15. The expert report prepared by the ECHR doctors was released in 2005. According to this report, forty out of forty-four people examined can live in prison conditions. See http://www.milliyet.com.tr/2005/07/06/son/sonsiy14.html.

16. Immediately after she submitted her thesis, Selen was appointed to a branch of the council outside Istanbul. Exasperated by the pressure at the council she experienced as she was writing her dissertation, she decided to quit her job.

17. Doctors, especially those who are affiliated with human rights organizations or the Turkish Medical Association, are knowledgeable about the health consequences of long-term hunger. As discussed in previous chapters, there were doctors such as Ata Soyer, Nusret Fişek, and Veli Lök, who took active roles in the anti-torture movement after the coup by being vocal about prisoners' health and the deleterious health impacts of prisons. They visited prisons with the permission of the Ministry of Justice and wrote observation reports on health-related problems of prisoners, including their access to health care. They wanted to understand how unhealthy living conditions in prisons, torture, and hunger strikes were interrelated and how they impacted the prisoners' health. These doctors have reflected on doctors' ethical responsibilities in times of a hunger strike. They also conducted research on the health consequences of a hunger strike as a political action (Soyer 1996).

18. The Turkish Medical Association has a very comprehensive list of documents regarding the role of physicians during hunger strikes as well as ethically proper medical attitudes and practices toward hunger strikers. The hunger strikers take a certain amount of water, salt, and sugar to prolong their hunger protest. The doctors informed them of the importance of taking B1 vitamins in order to protect their brains from the adverse effects of hunger. The 1996 death fast had taught the doctors that B1 deficiency caused Wernicke-Korsakoff syndrome to start very quickly. See the Turkish Medical Association's brochure on the health consequences of hunger strikes: https://www.ttb.org.tr/kutuphane/aclikgrevhek.pdf

19. Ata Soyer edited a comprehensive volume titled *Prison and Health* where he brought together all available research and surveys conducted on the health conditions of prisoners since the 1980s. Soyer discusses eleven cases of ill prisoners who asked for their release because of their illness. Nine of these release requests were met based on the medical reports prepared either by state hospitals or the CFM. This was far from reflecting the broader health problems of the prisoners. There were 498 ill prisoners who did not have proper access to medical treatment in 1997 (Soyer 1999).

20. See "Güler Zere hakkında Türk Tabipleri Birliği - Bilimsel Araştırma Kurulu raporu," *TTB*, August 26, 2009.

21. For more information on the specialization boards of the CFM, see İdari Yapı: İhtisas Kurulları', n.d., http://www.atk.gov.tr/adli-tip-ihtisas-kurulu.html.

22. See Korkut, "Adli Tıp Gecikiyor, Güler Zere İçin Hala Karar Veremiyor," *Bianet*, September 11, 2009.

23. According to an investigative report on the health care services provided to inmates in penal institutions by the Grand National Assembly of Turkey, Human Rights Investigation Commission in 2015, out of 3,663 applicants for the implementation of Article 16, 343 received affirmative reports from the CFM while 1,832 received negative reports, and 1,043 were waiting for documents to be processed. See the Grand National Assembly of Turkey Human Rights Inquiry Committee, Report on the Examination of Health Services Provided to Convicts and Detainees in Penal Institutions, 2015 (*TBMM İnsan Haklarını İnceleme Komisyonu, Ceza İnfaz Kurumlarında Hükümlü ve Tutuklulara Sunulan Sağlık Hizmetleri Hakkında İnceleme Raporu*).

24. See "Güler Zere Cezasını Hastanede Çekebilir," *Habertürk*, July 23, 2009.

25. See "Güler Zere Yaşayan Ölü Gibi," *Milliyet*, November 3, 2009.

26. See "Cumhurbaşkanı Gül Zere'yi affetti," *Hürriyet*, November 7, 2009.

27. See Zere, "Güler Zere"nin Mektubu Bu Kez Dışarıdan," *Bianet*, November 16, 2009.

28. See "Güler Zere Öldü," *Radikal*, 7 May 2009.

29. See Tuncer, "Türkiye"de haftada 5 hasta mahpus yaşamını yitiriyor," *Youtube*, June 5, 2018.

30. See the following news report for further examples: "Ramazan Özalp geciken tahliyesinden sonra ancak 4 ay yaşadı: 'Adalet' in ömür törpüsü," *Hapiste Sağlık*, 2014.

31. According to the data released by the Ministry of Justice in February 2017, 841 ill prisoners were waiting to be released despite having positive reports from the CFM. This number was 63 in 2013. In other words, in the last four years, there was a 1,235 percent increase in the number of prisoners waiting to be discharged. See "451 hasta mahpus hayatını kaybetti, 1086'sı ölümü bekliyor," *Evrensel*, May 8, 2017. It is also important to note that as of April 2022, there are 1,517 ill prisoners, 651 of them seriously ill according to the yearly reports of the Human Rights Association.

32. Bakırköy republican prosecutor's decision to decline the postponement of execution of sentence, dated August 19, 2013.

Chapter 5

1. This is according to a report of the Turkish Medical Association released on August 1, 2013. See "Göstericilerin Sağlık Durumları / The Health Status of the Demonstrators," *TTB*, August 1, 2013. https://www.ttb.org.tr/haberarsiv _goster.php?Guid=671fffa8-9232-11e7-b66d-1540034f819c.

2. Despite the high number of doctors who volunteered to help injured demonstrators, it does not represent all doctors. There are even some notorious incidents in which doctors did not properly treat injured protestors in hospitals. The case of Ali İsmail Korkmaz is the most well-known. See "Ali İsmail Korkmaz davası," *Amnesty*, February 3, 2014. https://www.amnesty.org .tr/icerik/ali-ismail-korkmaz-davasi.

3. Physicians for Human Rights has documented "86 attacks on 69 medical facilities and the deaths of 178 health care workers in 2014 alone." See http://physiciansforhumanrights.org/blog/documentation-vital-to-ending -attacks-on-health-care-workers.html.

4. The Turkish Medical Association was established in 1953 by law and designed as a corporatist body under the purview of the Ministry of Health. However, since the 1970s it has transformed into an independent nongovernmental organization with leftist leanings. Despite a politically diverse membership base, which represent 80 percent (83,000) of the country's doctors,

political and ideological discourse of Turkish Medical Association's ruling cadre draws on "universal values of the medical profession and a Marxian class analysis" (Yilmaz 2014, 181). The Turkish Medical Association's critiques of the AKP government during the Gezi protests should also be understood in terms of the ideological conflict between the government's conservative and neo-liberal policies and the Turkish Medical Association's reliance on pro-labor and secular ideologies.

5. The violation of medical neutrality is a war crime, a breach of the Geneva Conventions and humanitarian laws. However, protests and non-armed conflicts are not recognized in international humanitarian law, and conflicts that do not take place between different sovereign states are not covered by the Geneva Conventions. Hence international humanitarian medical organizations such as Doctors Without Borders (MSF) increasingly rely on medical ethics "which require medical personnel to deliver treatment to all individuals" rather than international humanitarian law and the protections of medical neutrality when defending their humanitarian activities (Kreisel 2007). The literature on medical humanitarianism shows that most global medical humanitarian interventions are assumed to take place in a safe zone (Fassin 2012).

6. A muezzin is a man who calls Muslims to prayer from the minaret of a mosque.

7. See also Aciksoz's (2015) discussion of local appropriations of the Hippocratic oath in the encounters with doctors and ordinary people in Turkey during and after the Gezi protests.

8. See Article 34 in the Law on Meetings and Demonstrations, No. 2911: https://www.mevzuat.gov.tr/mevzuat?MevzuatNo=2911&MevzuatTur=1& MevzuatTertip=5.

9. See "Sağlıkçılardan Gezi Parkı'nda 'Soruşturma protestosu,'" June 14, 2013. https://www.odatv4.com/guncel/saglikcilardan-gezi-parkinda-sorusturma -protestosu-1406131200-38658.

10. The quote is from Article 11 of the Health Services Fundamental Law, No. 3359.

11. There is a five-minute video taken by a reporter of the Dogan News Agency. See http://www.mynet.com/video/haber/gezi-parkinda-ele-gecen-ilaclar -sergilendi-1511199/.

12. See "11 Bin 155 Kişi 'Gazdan Etkinlendim' Dedi," *Bianet*, July 1, 2013. https://bianet.org/haber/11-bin-155-kisi-gazdan-etkilendim-dedi-148110.

13. "Taksim Dayanışması Biziz, Biz Buradayız!," *Taksim Dayanışma*, July 19, 2013. http://taksimdayanisma.org/taksim-dayanismasi-biziz-biz-buradayiz.

14. Here one can see the charts prepared by the Turkish Medicine Association regarding the health conditions of the demonstrators who were injured
May 31-August 1: http://www.ttb.org.tr/index.php/Haberler/veri-3944.html.

Conclusion

1. The peace process, also known as the "Solution Process" regarding the
Kurdish question, from 2012 to 2015 with its potential for Turkey's democra-
tization, was short-lived. The collapse of a temporary ceasefire between the
PKK and the Turkish state brought about an escalation in military clashes in
the Kurdish cities. The government sent military vehicles into civilian areas in
the southeast to eradicate Kurdish militants from residential areas. According
to a fact sheet prepared by the Human Rights Foundation of Turkey, between
August 16, 2015, and March 18, 2016, the state implemented a total of sixty-
three curfews in at least twenty-two districts of seven cities, affecting almost
1.6 million citizens. During these curfews, 310 civilians, including many children and women, lost their lives in these towns. The report also notes that
"at least 79 bodies are either waiting in the CFM to be identified or buried in
common graves and places that are unknown." Moreover, it states that "at least
180 civilians, whose information on how they died is obtained, lost their lives
while they were within the boundaries of their homes. 162 of these people
were killed due to opened fire or being hit by a missile, and 18 of them lost
their lives due to the direct stress effect of curfews on their health conditions."
"16 August 2015–18 March 2016 Fact Sheet," *TIHV*, March 22, 2016. https://
en.tihv.org.tr/curfews/16-august-2015-18-march-2016-fact-sheet/.

2. Historically the photographs and videos of state violence inflicted on
the Kurdish population or dissident groups played an important role in the
mobilization of Kurdish people and political activists against state violence.
However, these videos or photographs are usually taken by human rights
activists, international observers, and by Kurdish reporters (Bayram 2011)
and used effectively to arouse political sensibility among people. Although
the tradition of using visual evidence as evidence of state violence continues
among human rights groups and Kurdish and leftist political organizations,
we are increasingly witnessing that security forces are also taking and leaking
these images of violence and that the higher-level politicians are not likely to
condemn or deny such practices.

3. One of the notorious examples of this irreverent attitude to normalize
torture through graphic uses of force belongs to Süleyman Soylu, the then
minister of interior affairs. Attending the General Security and Struggle
Against Drugs meeting in 2018, he said: "No matter how much they condemn

me, it is the duty of the police to break a drug dealer's leg when he or she sees a dealer near a school. They can just put the blame on me. Doing what is necessary is the duty of police." This open check to violence came from the top government official who oversees the police force. By mobilizing the graphic metaphor of breaking the legs of drug dealers to recruit popular support for his policies, Soylu implicitly promises immunity to those police officers who inflict spectacular and illegal uses of force that can be classified as torture. "Minister of Interior Soylu Orders Police to 'Break Leg,'" *Bianet*, January 3, 2018. https://bianet.org/english/human-rights/192964-minister-of-interior -soylu-orders-police-to-break-leg.

4. "European court dismisses requests to lift curfews in Turkey's southeast," *Hurriyet Daily News*, January 13, 2016. http://www.hurriyetdailynews .com/european-court-dismisses-requests-to-lift-curfews-in-turkeys-southeast -93791.

5. The most recent example of this concerns the actions of İstanbul Police Headquarters' security manager during the pride march. The office of the governor refused to file an investigation regarding his excessive uses of force against protestors during the pride march on the grounds that the level of force he inflicted was proportionate. "İstanbul Valiliği, Hanifi Zengin›in uyguladığı şiddeti ‹orantılı› bularak soruşturmaya izin vermedi," *Birgün*, September 29, 2022. https://www.birgun.net/haber/istanbul-valiligi-hanifi-zengin-in -uyguladigi-siddeti-orantili-bularak-sorusturmaya-izin-vermedi-404393.

REFERENCES

Abramowitz, Sharon Alane, and Catherine Panter-Brick. 2015. *Medical Humanitarianism: Ethnographies of Practice*. Pennsylvania Studies in Human Rights. Philadelphia: University of Pennsylvania Press.

Aciksoz, Salih Can. 2015. "Medical Humanitarianism Under Atmospheric Violence: Health Professionals in the 2013 Gezi Protests in Turkey." *Culture, Medicine, and Psychiatry*, August, 1–25.

Adams, Vincanne. 1998. *Doctors for Democracy: Health Professionals in the Nepal Revolution*. Cambridge, UK: Cambridge University Press.

Agamben, Giorgio. 1998. *Homo Sacer: Sovereign Power and Bare Life*. Stanford, CA: Stanford University Press.

Akarsu, Hayal. 2018. "'Proportioning Violence': Ethnographic Notes on the Contingencies of Police Reform in Turkey." *Anthropology Today* 34 (1): 11–14.

Akarsu, Hayal. 2024. "'We're Tired of This Weber Guy!'—Force Experts, Police Reforms, and the Violence of Standardization." *American Anthropologist*, November 4, 2024. https://doi.org/10.1111/aman.28028.

Alessandrini, Anthony, Nazan Üstündağ, and Emrah Yıldız, eds. 2013. *JADMAG Issue 1.4 "Resistance Everywhere": The Gezi Protests and Dissident Visions of Turkey*. Tadween Publishing. http://tadweenpublishing.com/products/jadmag-issue-1-4-resistance-everywhere-the-gezi-protests-and-dissident-visions-of-turkey.

Amnesty International. 1985. *Turkey: Testimony on Torture*. London: Amnesty International Publications.

———. 1989. *Türkiye Raporları*. Alan Yayıncılık (Series) 111. Cağaloğlu, İstanbul: Alan Yayıncılık.

Anstett, Élisabeth, and Jean-Marc Dreyfus, eds. 2017. *Human Remains and Identification: Mass Violence, Genocide and the "Forensic Turn."* Reprint. Place of publication not identified: Manchester University Press.

Aragüete-Toribio, Zahira. 2022. "Introduction: Anthropologies of Forensic Expertise in the Aftermath of Mass Violence." *Social Anthropology* 30 (3): 1–18.

Aretxaga, Begoña. 2000. "A Fictional Reality: Paramilitary Death Squads and the Construction of State Terror in Spain." In *Death Squad: The Anthropology of State Terror*, edited by Jeffrey A. Sluka, 46–69. Philadelphia: University of Pennsylvania Press.

———. 2001. "The Sexual Games of the Body Politic: Fantasy and State Violence in Northern Ireland." *Culture, Medicine and Psychiatry* 25 (1): 1–27.

———. 2003. "Maddening States." *Annual Review of Anthropology* 32 (1): 393–410.

———. 2005. *States of Terror: Begoña Aretxaga's Essays.* Occasional Papers Series (University of Nevada, Reno. Center for Basque Studies); No. 10. Reno: University of Nevada.

Asad, Talal. 1997. "On Torture, or Cruel, Inhuman and Degrading Treatment." In *Social Suffering*, edited by Arthur Kleinman, Veena Das, and Margaret M. Lock, 285–308. Berkeley: University of California Press.

Aslan, Özlem. 2007. "Politics of Motherhood and the Experience of the Mothers of Peace in Turkey." Graduate Program in Political Science and International Relations Boğaziçi Üniversitesi.

Associated Press. 2014. "Turkey Doctors Say Police, Govt Harassed Them." *New York Times*, January 9, 2014. http://www.nytimes.com/aponline/2014/01/09/world/europe/ap-eu-turkey-doctors-under-fire.html.

Babül, Elif M. 2017. *Bureaucratic Intimacies: Translating Human Rights in Turkey.* Stanford Studies in Middle Eastern and Islamic Societies and Cultures. Stanford, CA: Stanford University Press.

———. 2020. "Radical Once More: The Contentious Politics of Human Rights in Turkey." *Social Anthropology* 28 (1): 50–65.

Bargu, Banu. 2014a. "Sovereignty as Erasure: Rethinking Enforced Disappearances." *Qui Parle: Critical Humanities and Social Sciences* 23 (1): 35–75.

———. 2014b. *Starve and Immolate: The Politics of Human Weapons.* New Directions in Critical Theory. New York: Columbia University Press, 2014.

———. 2016. "Another Necropolitics." *Theory & Event* 19 (1).

Bayram, Sidar. 2011. "Another Story of the Daily Circulation of Özgür Gündem: Affective Materiality." Master's thesis, Boğaziçi University.

Bekaroğlu, Mehmet. 2010. "12 Eylül Cezaevlerinden F Tiplerine: Bir Politik Psikoloji Projesinin Hikayesi (From September 12 Prisons to F-Type

Prisons: The Story of a Political Psychology Project)." *Türkiye Psikiyatri Derneği Bülteni* 13 (2): 33–36.

Biner, Zerrin Özlem. 2020. *States of Dispossession: Violence and Precarious Coexistence in Southeast Turkey*. 1st ed. Ethnography of Political Violence. Philadelphia: University of Pennsylvania Press.

Bornstein, Erica, and Peter Redfield. 2011. *Forces of Compassion: Humanitarianism Between Ethics and Politics*. 1st ed. School for Advanced Research Advanced Seminar Series. Santa Fe, NM: School for Advanced Research Press.

Boyer, Dominic. 2008. "Thinking Through the Anthropology of Experts." *Anthropology in Action* 15 (2): 38–46.

Brenneis, Don. 2006. "Reforming Promise." In *Documents: Artifacts of Modern Knowledge*, edited by Annelise Riles, 41–70. Ann Arbor: University of Michigan Press.

Brown, Wendy. 1995. *States of Injury: Power and Freedom in Late Modernity*. Princeton, NJ: Princeton University Press.

———. 2004. "'The Most We Can Hope For . . .': Human Rights and the Politics of Fatalism." *South Atlantic Quarterly* 103 (2): 451–63.

Can, Başak. 2019. "The Necropolitics of Documents and the Slow Death of Prisoners in Turkey." In *Turkey's Necropolitical Laboratory*, edited by Banu Bargu, 97–117. Democracy, Violence and Resistance. Edinburgh: Edinburgh University Press.

———. 2020. "Researchers' Vulnerability: The Politics of Research in Official Clinical Settings in Turkey." *American Anthropologist* 122 (2): 383–86.

———. 2022. "How Does a Protest Last? Rituals of Visibility, Disappearances Under Custody, and the Saturday Mothers in Turkey." *American Anthropologist* 124 (3): 467–78.

Carr, E. Summerson. 2010. "Enactments of Expertise." *Annual Review of Anthropology* 39 (1): 17–32.

Cihan, Ahmet, and Mehmet Çetin. 2011. *Süleyman Cihan: komünist bir önderin yaşamı*. 1. basım. Yaşam ve anılar dizisi. Sultanahmet/İstanbul: Belge Yayınları.

Cohen, Stanley. 2001. *States of Denial: Knowing About Atrocities and Suffering*. Cambridge, UK: Blackwell Publishers.

Crossland, Zoe. 2009. "Of Clues and Signs: The Dead Body and Its Evidential Traces." *American Anthropologist* 111 (1): 69–80.

———. 2013. "Evidential Regimes of Forensic Archaeology." *Annual Review of Anthropology* 42 (1): 121–37.

Csordas, Thomas J. 2004. "Evidence of and for What?" *Anthropological Theory* 4 (4): 473–80.

Darıcı, Haydar, and Serra Hakyemez. 2022. "Neither Civilian nor Combatant: Weaponised Spaces and Spatialised Bodies in Cizre." In *Turkey's Necropolitical Laboratory: Democracy, Violence and Resistance*, 71–94. Edinburgh University Press.

Das, Veena. 2004. "The Signature of the State: The Paradox of Illegibility." In *Anthropology in the Margins of the State*, edited by Veena Das and Deborah Poole, 225–53. School of American Research Advanced Seminar Series. Santa Fe, NM: School of American Research Press.

———. 2007. *Life and Words: Violence and the Descent into the Ordinary.* Berkeley: University of California Press.

Daston, Lorraine, and Peter Galison. 2007. "The Image of Objectivity." *Representations* 40 (1): 81–128.

Dindar, Cemal. 2010. "12 Eylül ve Psikiyatri (September 12 and Psychiatry)." *Türkiye Psikiyatri Derneği Bülteni* 13 (2): 30–32.

Dole, Christopher T. 2020. "Experiments in Scale: Humanitarian Psychiatry in Post-Disaster Turkey." *Medical Anthropology* 39 (5): 398–412.

Fassin, Didier. 2007. "Humanitarianism as a Politics of Life." *Public Culture* 19 (3): 499–520.

———. 2010. "Inequality of Lives, Hierarchies of Humanity: Moral Commitments and Ethical Dilemmas of Humanitarianism." In *In the Name of Humanity: The Government of Threat and Care*, edited by Ilana Feldman and Miriam Iris Ticktin. Durham: Duke University Press.

———. 2011. "The Trace: Violence, Truth, and the Politics of the Body." *Social Research: An International Quarterly* 78 (2): 281–98.

———. 2012. *Humanitarian Reason: A Moral History of the Present Times.* Berkeley: University of California Press.

———. 2013. *Enforcing Order: An Ethnography of Urban Policing.* English ed. Cambridge, UK: Polity Press.

Fassin, Didier, and Estelle d'Halluin. 2007. "Critical Evidence: The Politics of Trauma in French Asylum Policies." *Ethos* 35 (3): 300–329.

Fassin, Didier, and Estelle d'halluin. 2008. "The Truth from the Body: Medical Certificates as Ultimate Evidence for Asylum Seekers." *American Anthropologist* 107 (4): 597–608.

Feldman, Allen. 1991. *Formations of Violence: The Narrative of the Body and Political Terror in Northern Ireland.* Chicago: University of Chicago Press.

———. 1994. "On Cultural Anesthesia: From Desert Storm to Rodney King." *American Ethnologist* 21 (2): 404–18.

Fischer, Michael M. J. 2003. *Emergent Forms of Life and the Anthropological Voice*. Durham: Duke University Press.

Fortun, Kim. 2001. *Advocacy After Bhopal: Environmentalism, Disaster, New Global Orders*. Chicago: University of Chicago Press.

Foucault, Michel. 1978. *The History of Sexuality*. New York: Pantheon Books.

———. 1984. "Truth and Power." In *The Foucault Reader*, edited by Paul Rabinow, 1st ed., 51–75. New York: Pantheon Books.

Franklin, Sarah, and Celia Roberts. 2006. *Born and Made: An Ethnography of Preimplantation Genetic Diagnosis*. Illustrated ed. Princeton, NJ: Princeton University Press.

Givoni, Michal. 2011. "Beyond the Humanitarian/Political Divide: Witnessing and the Making of Humanitarian Ethics." *Journal of Human Rights* 10 (1): 55–75.

Glynos, Jason. 2001. "The Grip of Ideology: A Lacanian Approach to the Theory of Ideology." *Journal of Political Ideologies* 6 (2): 191–214.

———. 2011a. "Fantasy and Identity in Critical Political Theory." *Filozofski Vestnik* 32 (January): 65–88.

———. 2011b. "On the Ideological and Political Significance of Fantasy in the Organization of Work." *Psychoanalysis, Culture & Society* 16 (4): 373–93.

Glynos, Jason, and Yannis Stavrakakis. 2008. "Lacan and Political Subjectivity: Fantasy and Enjoyment in Psychoanalysis and Political Theory." *Subjectivity* 24 (1): 256–74.

Gök, Şemsi, ed. 1985. *1. Ulusal Adli Tıp Günleri (25- 28 June 1984)*. İstanbul: Temel Matbaacılık.

Gök, Şemsi, and Cahit Özen. 1982. *Adli Tıbbın Tarihçesi ve Teşkilatlanması (The History and Organization of Forensic Medicine)*. Istanbul: Matematik Araştırma Merkezi Baskı Atölyesi.

Goodwin, Charles. 1994. "Professional Vision." *American Anthropologist* 96 (3): 606–33.

Göregenli, Melek, and Evren Özer. 2010. *Medya ve Insan Hakları Örgütlerinin Verilerinden Hareketle 1980'lerden Günümüze Türkiye'de İşkence: Epidemiyolojik Bir Başlangıç Çalışması*. Vol. 70. Türkiye İnsan Hakları Vakfı Yayınları; Hamamönü, Ankara: Türkiye İnsan Hakları Vakfı.

Guilhot, Nicolas. 2012. "The Anthropologist as Witness: Humanitarianism Between Ethnography and Critique." *Humanity: An International Journal of Human Rights, Humanitarianism, and Development* 3 (1): 81–101. https://doi.org/10.1353/hum.2012.0002.

Gürbilek, Nurdan, 1993. *Vitrinde Yaşamak: 1980'lerin Kültürel Iklimi*. 2. basım. Cağaloğlu, İstanbul: Metis Yayınları.

Gusterson, Hugh. 1996. *Nuclear Rites: A Weapons Laboratory at the End of the Cold War*. Berkeley: University of California Press.

Hage, Ghassan. 2000. *White Nation: Fantasies of White Supremacy in a Multicultural Society*. Radical Writing. Annandale, New South Wales: Pluto Press.

Hajjar, Lisa. 2022. *The War in Court: Inside the Long Fight Against Torture*. Oakland: University of California Press.

Hakyemez, Serra. 2017. "Margins of the Archive: Torture, Heroism, and the Ordinary in Prison No. 5, Turkey." *Anthropological Quarterly* 90 (1): 107–38.

Hamdy, Sherine F., and Soha Bayoumi. 2016. "Egypt's Popular Uprising and the Stakes of Medical Neutrality." *Culture, Medicine and Psychiatry* 40 (2): 223–41.

Harper, Ian, Tobias Kelly, and Akshay Khanna. 2015. "Introduction." In *The Clinic and the Court: Law, Medicine and Anthropology*, edited by Ian Harper, Tobias Kelly, and Akshay Khanna, 1–26. Cambridge Studies in Law and Society. New York: Cambridge University Press.

Hermez, Sami. 2015. "When the State is (N)Ever Present: On Cynicism and Political Mobilization in Lebanon." *Journal of the Royal Anthropological Institute* 21 (3): 507–23.

Holt, Ed. 2014. "Health Professionals Targeted in Ukraine Violence." *The Lancet* 383 (9917): 588.

Hopgood, Stephen. 2013. *The Endtimes of Human Rights*. Ithaca: Cornell University Press.

Hopgood, Stephen, Jack Snyder, and Leslie Vinjamuri, eds. 2018. *Human Rights Futures*. Reprint ed. Cambridge, UK: Cambridge University Press.

Hull, Matthew S. 2012. *Government of Paper: The Materiality of Bureaucracy in Urban Pakistan*. 1st ed. Berkeley: University of California Press.

Hurriyet Daily News. 2013. "POLITICS—Turkish Deputy PM Claims Gezi Protesters Kissed at Istanbul Mosque Where They Took Refuge." http://www.hurriyetdailynews.com/turkish-deputy-pm-claims-gezi-protesters-kissed-at-istanbul-mosque-where-they-took-refuge.aspx?PageID=238&NID=59499&NewsCatID=338.

Jasanoff, Sheila. 1995. *Science at the Bar: Law, Science, and Technology in America*. Cambridge, MA: Harvard University Press.

Karaman, Emine Rezzan. 2016. "Remember, S/He Was Here Once: Mothers Call for Justice and Peace in Turkey." *Journal of Middle East Women's Studies* 12 (3): 382–410.

Kayaalp, Ebru. 2015. *Remaking Politics, Markets, and Citizens in Turkey: Governing Through Smoke*. Suspensions (Series). New York: Bloomsbury Academic.

Keenan, Thomas, and Hito Steyerl. 2014. "What Is a Document? An Exchange Between Thomas Keenan and Hito Steyerl." *Aperture*, March, 58–64.

Keenan, Thomas, and Eyal Weizman. 2012. *Mengele's Skull: The Advent of a Forensic Aesthetics*. Berlin: Sternberg Press.

Kelly, Tobias. 2012. *This Side of Silence: Human Rights, Torture, and the Recognition of Cruelty*. Pennsylvania Studies in Human Rights. Philadelphia: University of Pennsylvania Press.

———. 2015. "The Causes of Torture: Law, Medicine and the Assessment of Suffering in British Asylum Claims." In *The Clinic and the Court: Law, Medicine and Anthropology*, edited by Ian Harper, Tobias Kelly, and Akshay Khanna, 72–95. Cambridge Studies in Law and Society. New York: Cambridge University Press.

Klein, Naomi. 2007. *The Shock Doctrine: The Rise of Disaster Capitalism*. 1st ed. New York: Metropolitan Books/Henry Holt.

Knorr-Cetina, K. 1999. *Epistemic Cultures: How the Sciences Make Knowledge*. Cambridge, MA: Harvard University Press.

Kreisel, Johanna. 2007. "The Benghazi Six and International Medical Neutrality in Times of War and Peace." *Health Law and Policy Brief* 1 (2): 42–50.

Kruse, Corinna. 2016. *The Social Life of Forensic Evidence*. Oakland, CA: University of California Press.

Latour, Bruno. 1988. *Science in Action: How to Follow Scientists and Engineers Through Society*. Cambridge, MA: Harvard University Press.

———. 2004. "Why Has Critique Run Out of Steam? From Matters of Fact to Matters of Concern." *Critical Inquiry* 30 (2): 225–48.

———. 2010. *The Making of Law: An Ethnography of the Conseil d'État*. Cambridge, UK: Polity Press.

Leshem, Noam. 2015. "'Over Our Dead Bodies': Placing Necropolitical Activism." *Political Geography* 45: 34–44.

Maguire, Mark, and Ursula Rao. 2018. "Introduction: Bodies as Evidence." In *Bodies as Evidence: Security, Knowledge, and Power*, edited by Mark Maguire, Ursula Rao, and Nils Zurawski, 1–23. Durham: Duke University Press.

Matoesian, Greg. 2008. "Role Conflict as an Interactional Resource in the Multimodal Emergence of Expert Identity." *Semiotica* 2008 (January):15–49.

Mavioğlu, Ertuğrul. 2004. *Asılmayıp Beslenenler: Bir 12 Eylül Hesaplaşması.* Üçüncü basım. Babil Yayınları 41. İstanbul: Babil Yayınları.

Morris, Meghan L. 2022. "Property in Transition: Legal Fantasies, Land 'Reforms,' and Contracting Peace in Colombia." *American Anthropologist* 124 (1): 53–63.

Moyn, Samuel. 2010. *The Last Utopia: Human Rights in History.* Cambridge, MA: Belknap Press of Harvard University Press.

———. 2012. "Substance, Scale, and Salience: The Recent Historiography of Human Rights." *Annual Review of Law and Social Science* 8 (1): 123–40.

Navaro-Yashin, Yael. 2002. *Faces of the State: Secularism and Public Life in Turkey.* Princeton, NJ: Princeton University Press.

———. 2012. *The Make-Believe Space: Affective Geography in a Postwar Polity.* Durham: Duke University Press Books.

Nichanian, Marc. 2009. *The Historiographic Perversion.* New York: Columbia University Press.

Özkalıpçı, Önder, Ümit Şahin, Türkcan Baykal, Şebnem Korur Fincancı, Okan Akhan, Fikri Öztop, and Veli Lök. 2010. *Atlas of Torture: Use of Medical and Diagnostic Examination Results in Medical Assessment of Torture.* Ankara: Human Right Foundation of Turkey.

Ozsoy, Hisyar. 2010. "Between Gift and Taboo: Death and the Negotiation of National Identity and Sovereignty in the Kurdish Conflict in Turkey." PhD diss., University of Texas at Austin.

Patel, Geeta. 2007. "Imagining Risk, Care and Security: Insurance and Fantasy." *Anthropological Theory* 7 (1): 99–118.

Petryna, Adriana. 2002. *Life Exposed: Biological Citizens After Chernobyl.* In-Formation Series. Princeton, NJ: Princeton University Press.

Physicians for Human Rights. 2011. "DO NO HARM: A Call for Bahrain to End Systematic Attacks on Doctors and Patients." Report. Physicians for Human Rights.

———. 2013. *PHR Documents Improper Use of Tear Gas and Unnecessary Force on Demonstrators in Turkey.* http://physiciansforhumanrights.org /press/press-releases/phr-documents-improper-use-of-tear-gas-and -unnecessary-force-on-demonstrators-in-turkey.html.

Physicians for Human Rights (U.S.). 1996. *Torture in Turkey & Its Unwilling Accomplices: The Scope of State Persecution and the Coercion of Physicians.* Boston: Physicians for Human Rights.

Pişkinsüt, Sema. 2001. *Filistin Askısından Fezlekeye İşkencenin Kitabı.* Bilgi Dizisi 137. Ankara: Bilgi Yayınevi.

Puar, Jasbir K. 2017. *The Right to Maim: Debility, Capacity, Disability*. Durham: Duke University Press.

Ralph, Laurence. 2020. *The Torture Letters: Reckoning with Police Violence*. London: University of Chicago Press.

Redfield, Peter. 2006. "A Less Modest Witness." *American Ethnologist* 33 (1): 3–26.

———. 2013. *Life in Crisis: The Ethical Journey of Doctors without Borders*. Berkeley: University of California Press.

Robbins, Joel. 2013. "Beyond the Suffering Subject: Toward an Anthropology of the Good." *Journal of the Royal Anthropological Institute* 19 (3): 447–62.

Rose, Jacqueline. 1996. *States of Fantasy*. The Clarendon Lectures in English Literature. Oxford: Clarendon Press.

Rosenblatt, Adam. 2013. "Exhuming Equality: The Forensics of Human Rights." *Boston Review*, December 2, 2013. http://www.bostonreview.net /world/rosenblatt-mass-graves-exhumation-human-rights-forensics.

———. 2015. *Digging for the Disappeared: Forensic Science After Atrocity*. Stanford Studies in Human Rights. Stanford, CA: Stanford University Press.

Şahin, Doğan. 2010. "12 Eylül'le Hesaplaşma (Coming to Terms with September 12)." *Türkiye Psikiyatri Derneği Bülteni* 13 (2): 6–8.

Saluk, Seda. 2024. "Ethnography Under Authoritarianism: Notes from Medical Anthropological Fieldwork." *International Journal of Middle East Studies* 56 (1): 134–38.

Sayari, Sabri. 1987. "The Terrorist Movement in Turkey: Social Composition and Generational Changes." *Journal of Conflict Studies* 7 (1): 21–32.

Saymaz, İsmail. 2012. *Polisin Eline Düşünce Sıfır Tolerans*. Istanbul: İletişim.

Scarry, Elaine. 1985. *The Body in Pain: The Making and Unmaking of the World*. New York: Oxford University Press.

Scott, Joan Wallach. 2012. *The Fantasy of Feminist History*. Next Wave Provocations. Durham: Duke University Press.

Shapin, Steven, and Simon Schaffer. 1985. *Leviathan and the Air-Pump: Hobbes, Boyle, and the Experimental Life: Including a Translation of Thomas Hobbes, Dialogus Physicus De Natura Aeris by Simon Schaffer*. Princeton, NJ: Princeton University Press.

Silverstein, Brian. 2020. *The Social Life of Numbers: Statistics, Reform and the Remaking of Rural Life in Turkey*. Berlin: Palgrave Macmillan.

Smith-Nonini, Sandy. 2010. *Healing the Body Politic: El Salvador's Popular Struggle for Health Rights from Civil War to Neoliberal Peace*. New Brunswick, NJ: Rutgers University Press.

Songar, Ayhan. 1984. "Terrorism in General and Psychiatric Evaluation of Terroristic Events in Turkey." In *International Terrorism and the Drug Connection—Symposium on International Terrorism. 17–18 April 1984.* Ankara: Ankara University.

Soyer, Ata. 1993. *Önce insan olmak: insan haklari, Çevre, baris ve hekimlik üstüne.* Cağaloğlu, Istanbul: Belge Yayinlari.

———, ed. 1996. *Hekimlik ve insan hakları: Türk Tabibleri Birliği deneyimi, 1984–1992.* Türk Tabibleri Birliği yayını. Ankara: Türk Tabibleri Birliği.

———. 1999. *Cezaevi ve sağlık: cezaevi, ezaevi, sayrıevi, ölümevi.* Yenişehir, Ankara: Türk Tabibleri Birliği Merkez Konseyi.

Stavrakakis, Yannis, ed. 2020. *Routledge Handbook of Psychoanalytic Political Theory.* New York: Routledge.

Stoler, Ann Laura. 2002. *Carnal Knowledge and Imperial Power: Race and the Intimate in Colonial Rule.* Berkeley: University of California Press.

Sunder Rajan, Kaushik. 2006. *Biocapital: The Constitution of Postgenomic Life.* Durham: Duke University Press.

Taussig, Michael. 1984. "Culture of Terror—Space of Death. Roger Casement's Putumayo Report and the Explanation of Torture." *Comparative Studies in Society and History* 26 (3): 467–97.

Taussig, Michael T. 1997. *The Magic of the State.* New York: Routledge.

Ticktin, Miriam. 2010. "Where Ethics and Politics Meet." In *A Reader in Medical Anthropology: Theoretical Trajectories, Emergent Realities,* edited by Byron Good, 245–62. Chichester, West Sussex, UK: Wiley-Blackwell.

———. 2011. *Casualties of Care: Immigration and the Politics of Humanitarianism in France.* Berkeley: University of California Press.

———. 2014. "Transnational Humanitarianism." *Annual Review of Anthropology* 43 (1): 273–89.

Tuşalp, Erbil. 1986. *12 Eylül Tutanakları: Bin Tanık.* 1. baskı. Vol. 30. Dost Kitabevi Yayınları; Ankara: Dost Kitabevi yayınları.

Weizman, Eyal. 2012. *The Least of All Possible Evils: Humanitarian Violence from Arendt to Gaza.* London: Verso.

Weizman, Eyal, and Andrew Herscher. 2011. "Conversation: Architecture, Violence, Evidence." *Future Anterior: Journal of Historic Preservation, History, Theory, and Criticism* 8 (1): 111–23.

Wilcox, Lauren. 2011. "Dying Is Not Permitted: Sovereignty, Biopower, and Force-Feeding at Guantánamo Bay Document." In *Torture: Power, Democracy, and the Human Body,* edited by Shampa Biswas and Zahi Anbra Zalloua, 101–28. Global Re-Visions. Seattle: University of Washington Press in association with Whitman College, Walla Walla, WA.

Yilmaz, Volkan. 2014. "Health Reform and New Politics of Health Care in Turkey." PhD diss., University of Leeds. http://etheses.whiterose.ac.uk /7635/.

Yıldız, Kerim, and Juliet McDermott. 2004. *Torture in Turkey: The Ongoing Practice of Torture and Ill-Treatment.* London: Kurdish Human Rights Project.

Yoltar, Cagri. 2017. "The Politics of Indebtedness: The Dialectic of State Violence and Benevolence in Turkey." PhD diss. Duke University.

Yonucu, Deniz. 2018. "The Absent Present Law: An Ethnographic Study of Legal Violence in Turkey." *Social & Legal Studies* 27 (6): 716–33.

———. 2022. *Police, Provocation, Politics: Counterinsurgency in Istanbul.* Police/Worlds. New York: Cornell University Press.

Yörük, Erdem, and Murat Yüksel. 2014. "Class and Politics in Turkey's Gezi Protests." *New Left Review*, no. 89: 103–24.

INDEX

ACKNOWLEDGMENTS

I want to thank all the human rights activists and doctors that participated in my research. Their perseverance and dedication to their political and professional work continue to fascinate me. Only after spending many hours with them did I begin to realize how they could keep their spirits up despite working on violence, suffering, and torture. Even though I cannot put their names here, I will always feel grateful to them not only for their participation in this research but also for doing what they do with such commitment and passion.

I want to thank my mentors at Boğaziçi and Penn—Nazan Üstündağ, Nükhet Sirman, Meltem Ahıska, Philippe Bourgois, Adriana Petryna, and Deborah Thomas—who have each taught me to be creative, courageous, and critical in their own different ways. I have presented parts of this book on different occasions where I received helpful feedback from scholars and colleagues: Elif Babül, Banu Bargu, Niko Besnier, João Biehl, Omar Darwish, Didier Fassin, Onur Günay, Zeynep Gürsel, Susana Narotzky, Ayşe Parla, Nazan Üstündağ, Sertaç Sehlikoğlu, and Emrah Yıldız. I also want to thank my colleagues at Koç University including Dean Aylin Küntay, Fatoş Gökşen, Dikmen Bezmez, Can Nacar, Çetin Çelik, and İpek and Alexis Rappas for being supportive and collegial during the writing of this book. I thank the Wenner-Gren Foundation's Post-Hunt Fellowship and the Institute for Advanced Study at Princeton University for enabling the writing of this book with their generous support. Finally, I'm grateful to the University of Pennsylvania Press and my editors Jenny Tan, Lily Palladino, and Jill Twist for their invaluable support, expert guidance, and dedication in bringing this book to life.

Since my MA years, Nazan has always been a source of theoretical inspiration, teaching me how to be simultaneously generous and critical when understanding the world. Ergin read every single line of this manuscript. His unwavering belief in my potential often surpassed my own, providing me with the confidence to persevere. I am grateful to Erdem for convincing me to pursue a doctoral degree and for his continued support in both my academic and non-academic endeavors. I am lucky to have been surrounded with many good friends while writing this book, and I thank them all: Burak, İnanç, Yusuf, Onur, Mavcı, Barış, Gözde, Aslı, Sertaç, Murat, Mine, Zeynel. My dearest sisters, Ilgın, Çağrı, Pınar, Cansu ... Even if we can't see each other much, your presence in my life is invaluable. I feel grateful to have our small Istanbul group with Özgen, Gizem, and Samira, who always make me feel understood. I'm grateful to the members of my large family, my father-in-law Metin, my mother-in-law Gülizar, my aunts Özgün, Öznur, Asuman, Dilek, and Yaşar, my uncle Mehmet, and my cousins Senem, Esen, Koray, Murat, Çilem, Can, and Zafer for their support and love. Finally, I couldn't have written this book without my writing group with Nazan, Emrah, and Ergin. They gave me much needed motivation and encouragement at every stage of this book. I cannot thank them enough.

Lastly, I am grateful to my mom Özden, dad Çetin, and brother Önder for their unconditional support. I can never fully express how grateful I am for their love and care. Their kindness and dedication have shaped who I am today, and I feel incredibly blessed to have them in my life. Ergin, my husband, lover, and closest friend ... Every moment spent with you and our little son, Mahir, fills life with depth and purpose. Mahir's curiosity and wonder constantly inspire me to see things anew, while your presence gives me the strength and joy to navigate all of life's challenges. I can't imagine my life without the warmth, laughter, and strength you both bring.